ENGAGING
BABIES
IN THE LIBRARY

ENGAGING

BABIES

IN THE LIBRARY

Putting Theory into Practice

DEBRA J. KNOLL

ala
editions

An imprint of the American Library Association
CHICAGO 2016

DEBRA J. KNOLL is a former children's librarian and academic instructor. Her research has focused on the development of infants and toddlers and its implications for children's librarianship.

© 2016 by the American Library Association

Extensive effort has gone into ensuring the reliability of the information in this book; however, the publisher makes no warranty, express or implied, with respect to the material contained herein.

ISBNs
978-0-8389-1434-2 (paper)
978-0-8389-1445-8 (PDF)
978-0-8389-1446-5 (ePub)
978-0-8389-1447-2 (Kindle)

Library of Congress Cataloging-in-Publication Data

Names: Knoll, Debra J.

Title: Engaging babies in the library : putting theory into practice / Debra J. Knoll.

Description: Chicago : ALA Editions, an imprint of the American Library Association, 2016. | Includes bibliographical references and index.

Identifiers: LCCN 2015049312| ISBN 9780838914342 (print : alk. paper) | ISBN 9780838914458 (pdf) | ISBN 9780838914465 (epub) | ISBN 9780838914472 (kindle)

Subjects: LCSH: Children's libraries. | Libraries and infants. | Libraries and toddlers. | Libraries and families. | Children's libraries—United States. | Libraries and infants—United States. | Libraries and toddlers—United States. | Libraries and families—United States.

Classification: LCC Z718.1 .K63 2016 | DDC 027.62/5—dc23 LC record available at http://lccn.loc .gov/2015049312

Cover design by Karen Sheets de Gracia.

Text design by Alejandra Diaz in the Mrs Eaves, Gotham, and HWT Van Lanen typefaces.

♾ This paper meets the requirements of ANSI/NISO Z39.48—1992 (Permanence of Paper).

Printed in the United States of America

20 19 18 17 16   5 4 3 2 1

TO FAMILY . . . BECAUSE OF BEN

CONTENTS

ACKNOWLEDGMENTS

THIS BOOK OWES A TREMENDOUS DEBT TO THE MANY WHO CONTRIBUTED to the vision of a dedicated library space for infants, toddlers, and preschoolers and to those who truly believe in raising the bar for providing quality library service to this population. Appreciation is hereby extended to the community, staff, administration, and board of trustees of the Loudonville (Ohio) Public Library for trusting in, and allowing to happen, all the wonderful library opportunities you made possible for your children. A further note of gratitude is also extended to Susan Burwell, Eric Taggart, Charlie Hansen, Kimberlee Kiehl, Mary Mould, Diane Karther, Saroj Ghoting, Kathy East, Cindy Moseman, Alinde Moore, Les and Colleen Sandusky, and Janet Ingraham-Dwyer.

I am also deeply indebted to the many who were willing to listen to the dream, embrace its significance, and encourage its reality. A special thank you is extended to Kate Westfall, Helen Dupont, Carolyn Cooksey, Laura Leitner, Karen Archibald, Sheri Watkins, Lisa Weidner, Jeff Bell, Elaine Butts, Cody and Kati Jo Walters-Knoll, Nathan Westfall, and Philip Barber.

A note of thanks is also extended to the staff at ALA Editions, especially to editor Jamie Santoro.

And finally, a special mention of gratitude and appreciation is hereby extended to my colleague and friend Kristy Spreng, whose passion for children, unwavering conviction, ability to join in the shared vision of what is possible, and tenacity with which to see things through to completion are unsurpassed.

FOREWORD

THE *NEW YORK TIMES* RECENTLY FEATURED A STORY ON THE FRONT PAGE with the headline "Long Line at the Library? It's Story Time Again."[1] The author, Winnie Hu, reported a 28 percent increase in storytime attendance at New York City public libraries. We learn about library clerks pressed into duty as stroller parking attendants and about parents telling prospective nannies that they expect them to take their children to library storytime. Sari Feldman, president of the American Library Association, is quoted as saying that these enhanced story-times for very young children are part of a nationwide phenomenon of libraries transforming themselves into learning centers.

Anyone who has been working in or studying public libraries over the past decade or so has to have noticed the sea change in attitudes and services devoted to babies and toddlers. Many libraries have converted public space into places where very young children and their caregivers can find interactive games and educational toys ranging from play kitchens to puzzles and bead stringers. Board books are now standard additions to children's collections. Storytimes, as noted, have morphed into age-appropriate occasions for early literacy activities of all kinds with waiting lists of children whose caregivers are eager for them to attend. Stimulated and supported by Every Child Ready to Read, the curriculum developed by the Association for Library Service to Children and the Public Library Association, children's librarians have taken on the role of teaching parents how to be their children's first teachers and guiding caregivers about how to support those efforts.

Many manuals and guidebooks are now available to help librarians create early childhood play spaces and present enhanced storytimes that facilitate the learning of infants, toddlers, and preschoolers. In *Engaging Babies in the Library*, Debra Knoll adds the missing pieces to those practical handbooks. She provides well-researched tips and advice for dealing with the emotional needs and the often mystifying behavioral manifestations of those needs in babies and toddlers. Many librarians are comfortable in their roles as storytellers but a little less confident about interacting with a crying baby and her anxious mother standing at the reference desk while adults using the computers glare at them. What about the father who doesn't know what restroom he should use with his two-year-old daughter? Or the mother looking for a quiet, private place to nurse her newborn? Or the big brother who is clearly not happy with the arrival of an adorable sibling?

Knoll gives sensible, sensitive advice for all these situations and more. She provides clear time lines for the physical, emotional, intellectual, and social development of young children. Occasional sidebars help to bring developmental issues to life with anecdotes taken from real-life experiences in libraries. For readers who are inspired to implement this more holistic approach to service to these youngest patrons and their caregivers, she provides carefully constructed Baby Steps and Big Steps for each topical area.

All of us who care about children would stand up and cheer if all public libraries could take the Big Steps to ensure that babies and toddlers are served with the commitment and competence Knoll describes here. In fact, we would like to see *all* children, from birth through adolescence, served by librarians who have the expertise and resources to meet their physical, emotional, intellectual, and social needs. Debra Knoll herself acknowledges that this is a highly challenging goal right now. However, just having the vision articulated by her is a Baby Step toward achieving it.

—**Virginia A. Walter**
UCLA Department of Information Studies

Note

1. Winnie Hu, "Long Line at the Library? It's Story Time Again," *New York Times*, November 1, 2015, www.nytimes.com/2015/11/02/nyregion/long-line-at-the -library-its-story-time-again.html?_r=0.

INTRODUCTION

AT FIRST BLUSH, THE VERY IDEA OF COMBINING BABIES WITH LIBRARIES is somewhat oxymoronic—it would seem that they just don't go together. This sentiment is a carryover from the early days, when babies, children, and even teens were not only unwelcome, they were not *allowed* into libraries. Thankfully, those in the profession of children's librarianship championed their inclusion, and today's library culture enthusiastically welcomes them all. However, the long-ago prejudicial attitude that accompanied those outdated sentiments and former practices is still strongly influencing the way many families with babies and toddlers *perceive* the library. On the other hand, babies as library *patrons* is a relatively recent notion. It wasn't very long ago that, as a matter of policy, a child needed to be able to write his full name in order to be issued a library card. Now, some libraries are inviting newborns to acquire one.

Nevertheless, the profession is still grappling with what it means to serve babies and toddlers, along with their diverse family units, in the more general sense. Also, professionals are continuing to explore how to further encourage the development of pre- and early literacy skills, so important to the mission of librarians. As the profession has adapted over the years and has adopted literacy as one of its primary missions, it only makes sense to entice these families into what has long been perceived as the "no baby zone" of the public library. Finally, today's librarians are also being invited into the role of media mentor, wherein they are called upon to assist parents in using electronic devices positively in order to enrich and educate even the youngest members of our society. Bridges are being built all over the library landscape to broadcast that babies and toddlers, siblings, and caregivers all belong in the library. But what is the librarian's role and involvement once these new patrons arrive?

SERVING BABIES AND FAMILIES IN THE PUBLIC LIBRARY

There is much to consider if providing quality service to babies, toddlers, and caregivers is to be a goal of public librarianship. As *places* for these services to be encouraged and enriched, library spaces require careful thought. If such an area were to be developed, what would be the requisite features? How would it fit into the children's area as a whole? Because babies do not engage library spaces alone, what sorts of amenities, if any, should the library provide in this area for accompanying care providers? And babies often bring with them their preschool-age siblings. Do these siblings, too, have a place nearby? If so, what would be required in that additional space? If such a space were indeed to be created, what other problems might it attempt to solve? What would the entire process of creation and implementation entail? Who would build the space? And who would pay for it?

Extending children's librarianship services to babies, toddlers, and care providers would also need to be reexamined, perhaps to reevaluate priorities, goals, and practices. For example, the librarian would need to be familiar with infant and early childhood developmental processes. As one committed to the mission of children's services, the professional would also need to understand the earliest processes involved in emerging literacy skills. She would also need the skill to interact fluidly with each baby along with the care provider and any other accompanying family member, especially the toddlers and preschoolers who are also in various stages of rapid development along similar trajectories. How would this new service look, and how would it unfold in the daily activity in the library? How would it alter, extend, or change what is currently being practiced?

Answering these questions, solving any identified problems, and embracing the challenges they present to the profession is a very tall order. However, to do so, in very real terms and very real ways, has the potential to impact positively the lives of these baby patrons in very deep, brain-based ways, as well as to modify the direction of library space planning and applied librarianship. And embracing this challenge could truly alter for the better the course of the lives of children growing up in today's society. To seriously commit to this change and to fully address the challenges, taking steps to invoke a real sense of welcome is long overdue and, for many children today, *very* necessary. Although librarians have intuited this challenge for quite some time, they may be unclear about how to proceed.

HOW THIS BOOK CAN HELP

Engaging Babies in the Library focuses squarely on the *how* of providing quality library service to babies and families. There is no longer a question about *why*, as research continues to churn out supporting evidence of the vast learning that is occurring in babies and toddlers. As public institutions and entities, children's library spaces and the librarians who serve them have the unique opportunity to foster healthy growth and development for this population, promoting positive impact on a very broad scale. Embracing this challenge and including it in daily practice further advances the profession while also creating a stronger voice of advocacy for children. Win-win-win. Making these changes happen, however, is another thing altogether.

Chapter 1 tells the story of how one library and two librarians came to better understand what is involved in serving babies, toddlers, and care providers. Each of the next four chapters opens with a short discussion of differing aspects in the developing life of a baby. Chapter 2 addresses physical growth and associated needs. Chapter 3 discusses issues that arise as babies develop emotionally. Chapter 4 presents various components of the growing intellect. Chapter 5 addresses the importance and significance of social growth and exchanges.

The information presented in the Developmental Time Line sections is culled from several well-respected sources, including *Blackwell Handbook of Childhood Cognitive Development* and the highly respected Zero to Three: National Center for Infants, Toddlers, and Families website, which reports on and makes available original child development research.[1] The time line elements were chosen for their application to the profession. They were also chosen as a means to highlight how quickly a baby's brain develops and advances as well as perhaps to invoke a feeling of awe and respect for the various processes. The information provided in these pages does not pretend to cover the breadth, depth, or scope of all that the growing baby is experiencing and what ongoing research is illuminating. The discussions included in each chapter relate to how these developmental processes present themselves while the baby is visiting the library with his family.

The Baby Steps sections offer service tips and suggestions that librarians can easily or inexpensively adopt or implement. The Big Steps sections invite librarians to think creatively about what may be possible with further investment, support, funding, and collaborative efforts.

Chapter 6 begins with an overview of what the profession upholds as standard quality librarianship and how this concept may be interpreted in keeping with service to babies and families. The chapter concludes with a call to continue the conversation, to reignite the passion for fully including children—and babies—in libraries. The chapter charges the profession to transform policy and practice in ways that advocate for babies and families and to heed the call to make life better for them. The stories included are true, with names changed to protect privacy.

This book invites you to open, expand on, and continue conversations about ways in which children's librarians can rise to the challenge of providing quality service to babies, toddlers, and care providers. I also hope that the information in this volume can be used at the planning table to assist children's librarians in justifying their requests and suggestions for support, and for acquiring adequate funding and staff hours, as the investment in these lives promises so much in return. The book also emphatically encourages libraries to reevaluate children's library spaces and carve out a little bit of room for the library's littlest patrons, the babies, *along with* adequate spaces for their slightly older siblings and care-givers. Providing quality service to families with babies and toddlers presents its own unique challenges. Nevertheless, there is no portion of our society that is more important, more vulnerable, and more delightful to work with, and for whom our efforts will have the greatest positive impact—for many years to come.

Note

1. Usha C. Goswami, ed., *Blackwell Handbook of Childhood Cognitive Development* (Malden, MA: Blackwell, 2003); Zero to Three: National Center for Infants, Toddlers, and Families, www.zerotothree.org.

LIBRARIANSHIP FOR BABIES

From Problems to Potential

HE VILLAGE OF LOUDONVILLE IS BEAUTIFULLY SITUATED IN the rolling landscape of northeastern Ohio, at the southernmost tip of Ashland County. The Loudonville Public Library is not only the pride of but also the center of activity in this small, rural community. As is common, this little village has become economically challenged, with jobs and services continuing to close and migrate to the larger cities and towns nearby. The library's patron base includes those of the Amish and Mennonite traditions, and the library is the frequent destination for a bustling home-school population. The meandering Mohican River edges the west side of town and flows southeastward through one of the largest camping and canoeing areas in the state. Because the broader area surrounding the village receives sketchy Internet and phone service, residents and tourists alike frequently use the library for Internet access as well as for informational and recreational purposes.

The children's department of the Loudonville Public Library is a lively place. Two full-time children's librarians were providing services to the children in the community when the subject of providing service to babies, and by extension their care providers, really began to be considered. We were also trying to stay abreast of the recent initiatives coming from within the profession about assisting parents in the task of raising readers. If babies and toddlers are indeed experiencing substantial brain growth and development, what could we do to better serve and assist them? Most of the focus of these initiatives remained on the slightly older three- to five-year-olds. We sensed the need was intense, but the way to proceed remained elusive.

PROBLEMS AT THE LOUDONVILLE PUBLIC LIBRARY

One day a gentle yet seismic shift began in our thinking as a result of a simple question. Tabitha, the mother of two boys, one about two years old and the other a three-month-old, asked, "Is there somewhere in the library where I can go to nurse my son?" Oddly enough, the answer was "No, not really." Yes, there were soft, comfy chairs, and the mother was invited to use those, but they were in immediate view of the circulation desk. She was fine with that but sensitive enough to be concerned about the comfort level of the elderly couple at the checkout counter nearby. She was then invited to use a small study room in the adult section, but because she had a toddler in tow, she didn't want to "invade" that space. Hmm. A temporary fix was put in place, and a rather chagrined pair of children's librarians began to explore ways to solve the problem—and consider the need.

As thoughts and conversations continued, other issues began to be identified and better defined. For example, there were problems for the families of babies and toddlers. There was no cohesive place to congregate, and caregivers and playmates seemed to be all over the place. The noise, clutter, and activity were situated near the center of the library, alongside the circulation area, making it difficult to contain enthusiastic yet perfectly normal outbursts of excitement or emotion. Such eruptions often led to discomfort or embarrassment on the part of parents, who then felt the need to extend unnecessary apologies to staff. Infants in carriers were frequently seen resting on the floor right in the middle of general foot traffic, posing a safety hazard for all. Also, mixed-age groups contended for space, with toddlers and upper elementary school–age children in the same area, causing frequent clashes.

The adult computer workstation was over *there*, the AWE children's educational computer workstation was forty feet over *there*, and a designated play area for preschool-age children was yet another forty feet over *there*, with no clear sight lines. The family, by virtue of the library's interior layout, was forced to split up into separate parts of the building, so the adults were unable to closely monitor their children's activities. The placement of the various computers also led to unattended-child situations or created infant- or toddler-oriented, low-level distractions in the adult area. And, because the computers faced away from the open room, it was difficult for care providers to keep their children in sight.

The children's librarians were also grappling with problems. Trying to provide quality service for the entire children's area basically amounted to crowd control. How was this working in conjunction with meeting professional goals, delivering information, and fostering pre- and early literacy skills? Frustration was mounting. Yet another specialized committee, task force, or workshop was being formed. Yes, we knew that these issues were important. We truly wanted to be agents of change. But what could we *do*? More of the same efforts obviously wasn't enough. The situation for the children was made even more urgent when statewide funding cuts resulted in reduced staff hours in the children's department. Now the librarians had to solve the problem of providing quality service to this population even as staffing, funding, and support for programming opportunities began to evaporate.

As time marched on and babies graduated into toddlers and then preschoolers, the sense of urgency to do something became stronger. We went searching for the perfect solution. Surely some library somewhere had it all: a place for infants to have access to books and be free to move about *and* an adjoining area for appropriate toddler and preschool play *and* a place for an adult to nurse a baby or access an Internet workstation—all at the same time. However, what we envisioned couldn't be found within the known library environments that were investigated. Although many beautiful children's library areas existed with a focus on play and literacy as well as places that allowed babies to crawl around a little, a sense of cohesiveness in providing spaces and services for the entire family package was lacking.

We took our search for the ideal space outside the world of libraries and found inspiration by visiting children's museums. These museums are typically devoted to creating opportunities for children to explore learning environments that highlight science and technology. We were looking for ways to meld the concept of contained educational play with appropriate library conduct and interactivity that enhanced overall development and fostered pre- and early literacy skills. In a startling moment of lucidity, it came to us to reverse the order of operations. Structured "pretend" libraries are available in children's museums to assist children in learning about science. Maybe we could create a small museum-like structure that could be incorporated into the library, with the goals of fostering general healthy development and encouraging emerging pre- and early literacy skills! Perhaps, too, with the right design, some of the other problems we had identified could be addressed.

Consultation with children's museum designers helped to bring more focus and clarity to our thinking. First, the Institute of Museum and Library Services *does* include children's libraries, confirming our conviction that a well-planned, museum-like structure might have a justified place in libraries. Second, we reflected on the profession itself, recognizing that library services should not be limited because of age. Therefore, children's librarians should provide access to books by the babies themselves. We also wanted to incorporate components that would encourage pre- and early reading development. And we wanted to entice nonusers into the library. We could see how this simple solution could address many of these challenges and solve existing space issues and problems. Finally, we needed a clear, overarching philosophy on which to ground our thinking. As we reflected on and discussed the physical, emotional, intellectual, and social components of child development, we determined that, much to our surprise, our ultimate goal was to create an environment that would foster developing social interactions and skills. All the other aspects of development fell into place as secondary, natural outcomes of this goal.

With our imaginations in high gear, we began to picture a beautifully rendered space just for babies. The area, by design, would also gently transition to allow for toddler play, and then on into a section devoted to preschooler pretend play. The area would provide babies with a safe space where they could move about, out of their carriers, allowing access to materials that are published specifically for them. It would include a few research-based pre- and early literacy interactive components. The general area would also include basic amenities for the care-providing adult, who could discreetly nurse a baby or access an Internet workstation and still be able to monitor the activity and whereabouts of older children. The location was to be separate from the general service area, where noise and clutter would be contained and disruptions to the public curtailed. This envisioned play space in the library would be intentional, permanent, and aesthetically pleasing, thus sending an intrinsic message of respect for and welcome to this population, hopefully reaching nonusers. It would be available to all families any time the library doors were open and would level the social playing field by serving the neglected child as well as the child who is doted upon.

THE DREAM BECOMES A REALITY

The building and installation of the Early Literacy Play Space (ELPS) took quite a long time to accomplish. The project faced the typical variety of challenges, such as others' inability to grasp the goals and concepts, resistance to change, lack of funding, and a rapid turnover in administration. As we sought ways to carve out room for the installation of such a space, a few hard decisions had to be made. The housing of magazines, paperback books, and a small reference section had to be reconsidered, reallocated, or downsized. All in all, despite space limitations and with a bit of creative reallocation, room was made, and with little overall collateral damage to existing collections.

The project was broken down into three stages. The first and most urgent step was to develop the baby area because babies had the least in the way of developmentally appropriate space and yet were learning and growing the most rapidly. Funding was gained through the generous contributions of local community members, foundations, and service organizations. A library design team was hired, and, after several discussions and planning sessions, building commenced. From the moment this first stage of the space was complete, we knew we were on to something. The area became much more than the sum of its parts, as families immediately occupied and enjoyed the space. It fairly pulsed with welcome, while stimulating interactions among a variety of age ranges and abilities. Because the area was so suitable for their holistic needs, families were often inclined to remain in the library for long periods, thereby extending healthy developmental interactions and play. To our surprise, creation of the space also expanded the very practice of librarianship in that we, as librarians, could encourage, engage in, and expand these play experiences. These abilities, in turn, ushered in a new way of thinking about the future of the profession itself and about what quality librarianship for this population really entails.[1]

The second stage of the project was to design and construct a computer workstation. It would allow an adult to sit next to a preschooler who could also engage in instructional, computer-related activity with grown-up assistance nearby. Elegantly designed and constructed by a team of local builders, and with exquisite attention to details that were meant to passively educate and encourage play, the "ticket booth" component was happily received. For many adults, its availability invokes a sense of relief as they can attend to what they need to do and still have their toddler children engrossed in play nearby, away from less tolerant adults. The slightly raised platform on which the workstation sits allows for slightly better visibility into the area. And there is room enough for an infant in a carrier to be set down and not be in the middle of foot traffic. Success, in that more problems were solved!

The third and final piece, more in keeping with the museum-like structure described earlier, was by far the most challenging to design and construct. Because the component was to be a structure more in keeping with a children's museum, we sought out a local company known for its efforts to create interactive learning environments and museum structures. Company leaders found the idea intriguing and were willing to tackle the construction of what we had envisioned—a challenge to build, indeed, because the unit, although very compact, contains numerous pre- and early literacy skill—enhancing components and pretend-play opportunities.[2] As the developing infants quickly grow into toddlers and then preschoolers, they are gently invited to play in more sophisticated ways, always with a mild emphasis on pre- and early literacy—enhancing activity. The entirety of the ELPS fits into a twenty-by-thirty-foot area toward the back of the children's department. (For more information, see note 2.)

The ELPS was instantly popular and continues to be so. As families become familiar with the area, they are quickly drawn to it and, somewhat amusingly, once through the library's door, hurry to get "back there" with their little ones. Also, many of the problems identified have been addressed and successfully resolved. The ELPS is frequently a go-to place for mothers, grandparents, campers, and others, all looking for somewhere to go to "get out of the house," "come in from the rain," or "find relief from the heat." Social exchanges, so very important to this population, are more easily conducted, as parents and caregivers gather in the area, meet for the first time, plan play dates, share stories, offer encouragement to each other, and otherwise find a place to just relax. And for many members of the community, there is no "entry fee" prohibiting use. The public library is still free and open to all.

One of the primary successes of the play space is that it is indeed inviting to those who usually do not use the public library. Loudonville is a small town, and we know our patrons fairly well. Since the inclusion of this space, we see new faces regularly as previously nonusing families are spreading the word about the library and its sense of welcome as a place for babies and toddlers. As time has gone by, the area has also been used in ways unanticipated. For example, the area has been identified by behavioral intervention specialists as a neutral place to meet with families and practice new skills. It has also been used for conducting gentle physical therapy exercises for children with disabilities. It has been identified as a safe, neutral place for supervised parental visitations. And it is used as an observation area for students studying infants and toddlers in a natural environment at various stages of development. The caregivers love the go-to area, the children are greatly benefited and have a grand time at play, and the librarians are deeply gratified by having so many problematic issues resolved. The community of Loudonville entrusted its librarians with this challenge, believed in the dream, and backed it with the funding necessary to make real change happen. The dream became reality—ideas came together, space was built, and the public was invited into this special environment. And it worked.

THE ELPS AND LIBRARIANSHIP

From a simple request to nurse a baby, to the conception of how to best alter spaces for this population, to the concrete reality of the ELPS, seven years passed. During those long years of laboring over the different stages of the project, the understanding and practice of what librarianship means to this population continued to unfold, evolve, and define itself. For example, as families gravitated to their area, they often created the perfect scenario for an impromptu story, song, or puppet play. As babies played, the librarians were able to just hover about, marveling at what they were observing and, in doing so, gently informing and inspiring caregivers. By extension, opportunities to draw attention to the Every Child Ready to Read initiative's educational components naturally arose within these social exchanges. The overall service model became much more fluid and holistic, assisting all these patrons simultaneously.

Furthermore, as we delved into infant and early childhood research studies, serendipitous observations of babies in the library reemphasized what researchers were reporting, expanding our sensitivity to and appreciation for what babies were attempting to accomplish. For example, we would watch an infant just learning to walk, maintaining his balance with his entire body trembling with exertion, gleeful, while holding a book in an effort to present it to his mommy. This simple exchange demonstrated his efforts to move about (physical development) and delight in his success (emotional expression). It also demonstrated his attempts to communicate (intellectual growth) and share with his adult (social exchange). We could now better appreciate how these simple encounters, easily overlooked in the past, were revealing the complex learning that was happening in baby's brain. We were learning that it was perhaps more appropriate to congratulate baby for his stunning success than to simply applaud him for his adorably executed gestures and efforts.

We were also introduced to a higher form of advocacy specific to this population. Even as we were studying these magnificent brain growth and development processes, we were made more aware of the serious challenges to healthy outcomes many members of this population are facing in today's social and cultural contexts. The vast potential of a child's gain in (or lack of) brain growth became a much more vital concern (see the feature "The Beauty of the Developing Brain"). Because children's librarians serve every child, we began to take more

The Beauty of the Developing Brain

As baby plays on her tummy at the library, she is fully absorbed in isometric exercise, with head and legs raised and arms outstretched to maintain balance. A stranger, the librarian, approaches. Baby darts a quick glance over to mother to gauge mother's reaction and is assured that this stranger is welcome. The librarian presents baby with a board book. Reaching toward it with fascination throws baby's whole body off balance, and she quickly adjusts to the situation. She adapts her strategy, grapples with the book, and rolls to her back so she can have a closer look. The entire episode transpires in seconds. This mild, routine interaction with the librarian illustrates many things. It demonstrates to baby's mother that the librarian acknowledges and values their visit, it introduces baby to a pre-literacy enriching event, and it opens the door for future social exchanges, as baby recognizes the librarian as a safe "other" in her growing social world.

The seemingly minor event of a baby grasping for a book illustrates the exquisite interplay of the various aspects of development that converge to create a foundation on which the baby will continue to grow. Each child is developing in physical, emotional, intellectual, and social ways, and these separate features of development, teased out, make it possible to discuss them in manageable ways, but baby brain growth occurs holistically, dynamically, and in very sophisticated patterns. Like a slowly turning kaleidoscope, every little exchange and interplay present yet another stunningly beautiful example of the elegance of this phenomenon.

affirmative steps to get the word out that babies and toddlers belong in the children's library, perhaps urgently so. This book is an outgrowth of the many discoveries and deepened convictions we experienced. What started out as an effort to solve many of the problems associated with serving babies, toddlers, and care providers ultimately brought about an entirely new way of perceiving this population and invited the opportunity to modify what it means to deliver respectful, quality library service.

The whole idea of creating a space that everyone could enjoy together seems so very simple. It is doable and *necessary*. It doesn't require a great deal of space, although larger libraries could certainly entertain that idea. Furthermore, the initial investment in a well-planned play area, relatively speaking, really isn't that expensive when considering the many years of service it will provide and the hundreds of lives that potentially will benefit in very deeply embedded, brain-based ways. Indeed, some libraries may struggle with how to alter existing environments, but there are still ways in which even minor modifications to existing spaces can help. Making sure that outlets are covered and sharp corners are addressed is an excellent first step, as is making provisions for babies to independently move about and access books.

A professional librarian, sensitive to the interchanges that are transpiring between, say, a toddler and a care provider, and then offering a tissue to soothe a tear-streaked face, may be making a seemingly small contribution, but that very gesture sends a message of comprehension of and respect for this group. By investing even little pieces of time and attention in these individuals, children's librarians have the opportunity to add their own unique influence on these developing little brains.

As the library profession is quite aware, it is sometimes very necessary to make a radical shift in approaching and implementing services in order to apply research findings, to maintain relevancy, and to follow cultural shifts. The discussions in the following chapters came about as a result of studying babies in action, by directly observing how research bears itself out in real time, and by making small advances into the world of babies. The discussions are offered in an effort to further explore thinking about this vulnerable group and to encourage librarians to consider just how very meaningful service to babies, toddlers, and their families can be.

Notes

1. Library Design Associates, www.librarydesign.com/contact.html.
2. Loudonville Public Library, www.loudonvillelibrary.org; Splashmakers, www.splashmakersllc.com/Splashmakers_LLC/Splashmakers_LLC.html.

PHYSICAL NEEDS
Attending to Babies and Families

THE HUMAN GROWTH PROCESS IS MOST READILY PERCEIVED by onlookers as a physical event. Infancy and toddlerhood, by their very definitions, imply maturation and change. After all, it is easy to see that babies gain weight, grow taller, teethe, become stronger, and learn to sit up. Of course, the growing process is attended by physiological consequences, such as slobbering, spitting up, burping, eliminating, and crying. The care provider must be prepared to meet these fundamental needs no matter what the setting. Wiping tears, catching spit-up, diapering, potty training, and tending to all the other physical events are part of the child development package.

The physiological developmental processes that babies and toddlers are experiencing, along with the adult's ability to provide adequately for those needs, are a reality and simply must be addressed. The adult's physical abilities, limitations, and self-care requirements must also be taken into consideration. After all, baby, toddler, and adult are coming to the library *together*. A welcoming environment respects these conditions and strives to make adequate provisions for this population. The efforts on the part of the library as a place in which these things occur, and by the librarian who understands, respects, and accepts this reality, are a fundamental component in welcoming families with babies into the library. Moreover, making basic provisions in these ways sends the message that babies and toddlers are *supposed* to come to the library and that their care providers will be able to adequately attend to them as well as to themselves.

PHYSICAL GROWTH: THE DEVELOPMENTAL TIME LINE

Two years in the life of an adult is quite different from two years in the life of a developing newborn. Whereas most adults would comment about the passage of time in such phrases as "where does the time go?" or "it seems like only yesterday," for the developing baby and toddler, time is experienced as very long, during which much change occurs. For the adults caring for these little ones, it is a unique season filled with many demands. Even as the time flies by, it sometimes feels like a long, long string of endless days of service and sacrifice. As the saying goes, time spent rearing children goes by "like an instant and an eternity."

Just what is physically transpiring during this time in a child's life? The baby, born with a variety of reflexes such as crying, sucking, and grasping, will soon be capable of movement with intention and volition. The newborn is also incredibly nearsighted and sees objects best at about eighteen inches from her face, just about the same distance as when daddy is cradling her in his arms. As the eyes take in such phenomena as color, light, and darkness, the muscles in and around the eyes are strengthening and learning to work together. She is learning that those flailing objects in her peripheral vision are her very own arms that she will soon bring under control. In only a few short weeks, the infant will develop the muscle strength needed to lift her head to look about. She will soon kick at will to watch the crib mobile dance. She finds her mouth with her hands. Soon she will be rolling over from back to tummy and from tummy to back by her own volition. By three to four months she will have progressed to the point of controlling the muscles necessary to construct an intentional smile.

By four months, baby will be working to master eye-hand coordination and will assist in holding her bottle. She will also begin the uncomfortable process of cutting teeth. Baby will start to master the various balances necessary to sit up, first with support, then unassisted. She will discover her feet and toes and delight in them. By six or seven months, she will actively assist in being carried about, clinging to whomever she is riding. She is becoming mobile, exercising and developing trunk and thigh muscles, as she attempts to scoot or even begin to crawl.

By around eight months or so, baby will master the thumb and finger pincer grip, making it possible for her to pick up very tiny objects, such as little crackers, carpet threads, beads, and bugs. She will crawl with a destination in mind, begin to pull up to a standing position, cruise along on two feet while holding on to supports, and eventually take that first step. Even as early as this eight-month stage, baby will select a favorite book and explore it using the fine motor activity needed to lift flaps, examine tactile elements, or otherwise manipulate the book.

The twelve-month-old, if she hasn't already done so, will be walking, or walking very soon, and then, of course, running—fast. She delights in the movement of her body and shows it by climbing, jumping, hurling, twirling, clapping. She delights her care providers by making awkward dance movements, mostly with feet planted on the floor. She is also learning how to blow kisses, bubbles, and candle flames, exhibiting knowledge of and limited control over her own breath. Soon the developing baby-turned-toddler will master balancing on one foot, hopping, executing stairs, and other more sophisticated forms of gross motor movement. She will also finesse such fine motor activity as making marks with a crayon, stacking blocks, and using thumbs in the correct position to text on toy cell phones.

The newborn has traveled a great distance in only a few short months. The brain is more active at this time than at any other in the human life span, busily making all those connections in its various regions to assist baby in understanding and mastering her physical body, as well as how things operate in the world. One of the most important means by which these basic skills are attained is practice. Movement, therefore, is crucial. When she is in the library, baby must have the opportunity to crawl toward, reach for, and otherwise arrive at the board books that are available to her. If this opportunity is not provided to her, she may spend most of her time at the library strapped in a carrier, in effect cut off from her method of interacting with the book collection intentionally acquired for her use—a contradiction, to be sure.

Babies and toddlers, all the way up through preschoolers, come to the library with more holistic physical needs than do older children and adults. Adults as readers, information seekers, or computer users are typically attending to passive tasks, such as browsing the shelves, perusing a magazine, surfing the Internet, or reading the paper. Children, especially the youngest ones, are active, physical *doers* while conducting their form of research and therefore require a very different use of space. Even this cursory overview of the many physical accomplishments that are being mastered during these first several months bears this out. Providing adequate spaces for these many developing processes, therefore, is *necessary*. However, it is also a very real challenge in the library setting. Part of the question most libraries face is not only *how* but also *where* and *how much*. After all, there is only so much real estate with which to work. However, an adequately planned area, even in somewhat tight quarters, holds great potential. To ignore its inclusion is to channel services for infants and toddlers through their care providers, denying those very infants and toddlers the right to choose for themselves the materials that may be of interest to them. Exclusion also marginalizes what the professional children's librarian can do and be for these patrons—such a librarian is severely limited in making meaningful interactions and connections as the little one will most likely remain confined and restrained.

BRAVING THE DOOR

The very idea of bringing a baby into a library can create a certain amount of anxiety for all involved. Babies, of course, cannot enter a library on their own. They must be carried into the facility and cared for while there, implying, of course, an attending parent or care provider. And even though they are very small, babies require a lot of equipment in our society. Here comes the baby, in a coat and hat, wrapped warmly in a blanket or two, a pacifier securely attached to his garment, "lovie" toy in hand. Snugged in a portable car seat, he is carted in by mom. Mom is also hauling a rather large, bulky diaper bag loaded with equipment and solutions to any conceivable contingency. Mom has tried to remember everything: cell phone, car keys, wallet, phone charger, feminine hygiene products, diapers, a few changes of clothes for the baby, a bottle or two, snacks, wipes, hand sanitizer, an extra "binky" just in case, a burp cloth, changing pad, toys, and any number of other necessities.

Also in tow is baby's two-year-old sibling, still in diapers, wearing a coat, hat, scarf, and mittens, and requiring more diapers and perhaps an "emergency" garment (also in the bag). And then there's mom's coat, scarf, hat, and gloves. It takes a lot, maybe a whole lot, of energy to gather all the stuff as well as the children, to pack everything and everyone in, and go. Likely mom is sleep deprived. Just making it from home to car, through traffic, and from car to building is no small feat. And as impossible as it may sound, mom will also heroically be carrying a book bag in which, she hopes, she placed everything that is due to be returned. Her timing, too, must be impeccable—between naps so that the children's best behavior can be anticipated.

The complete package can be quite heavy and cumbersome. And rarely quiet, especially when excited sibling toddlers and preschoolers are also involved! Librarians and support staff with even a modest understanding of human development are expected to tolerate (yet place boundaries on) rowdy, rambunctious teenagers bursting through the door. They also deal sympathetically with a shouting adult struggling with hearing loss. So, too, staff members and librarians, respecting the efforts being made by a family with young children just to brave the door, will want to alleviate any self-consciousness that the caregiver may feel. Just this simple courtesy can go a long way toward providing a sense of welcome and will likely encourage return visits. It bears mentioning that if the already self-conscious family members are met with deprecation or condescension, they will most likely not want to risk a return visit, implying lifelong ramifications for the developing baby.

Many parents, in an effort to get things off to a healthy start, make the library one of their first destinations. Some have *never* been to the public library. Some have been to the library only to borrow DVDs and have no idea what is there for babies, toddlers, and children. All feel somewhat hesitant and uncertain about how today's library visit will turn out.

Baby Steps

- Tolerate the noise associated with clamoring into the building. A certain level of noise is to be expected.
- Offer a warm greeting at the door as the family entourage enters.
- Post signs of welcome and direction.
- Recruit volunteer door greeters who can direct and assist families.
- Encourage support staff to recognize babies accompanying care providers and to direct or invite them to the children's section.
- If the children's area is far removed from the entry doors, perhaps a call to the children's staff members is in order so that they can meet the family and accompany everyone to the appropriate space.
- During staff training sessions, ask a few willing staff members to role-play a mother entering the library with two or three young children. Modify the situation: make it her first visit, have her check things out and exit, make the caregiver the dad or a physically challenged grandparent, and so on. Encourage dialogue and discussion.
- Host a staff training session specifically on this topic, inviting further discussion about providing physical service to families.
- Dedicate a few parking spaces that are a bit wider than the standard size so carriers, strollers, bags, car doors, children, and care providers can all maneuver between vehicles.

Big Steps

- When planning a building overhaul or a new structure, consider creating separate entrances, hallways, or corridors that will steer the family package into the children's area without having to navigate through main library service areas.
- Conduct research studies on the physical comfort level of parents of young children visiting the library, focusing particularly on perceptions of public library visits by families with babies and toddlers. Use the findings to adjust or adapt services, advertising, and policies.

MANAGING DOORWAYS, ELEVATORS, STAIRWAYS, AND STROLLERS

Since the implementation of the Americans with Disabilities Act of 1990 (ADA), public buildings have become much more accommodating. Installing such amenities as elevators and ramps makes wheelchairs, power chairs, and even strollers possible, thus serving the families with young children very well—sometimes. For example, automatic entry doors are useful, convenient, and even necessary. They assist the wheelchair-bound, those maneuvering strollers, and even staff members bringing supplies and book carts in and out of the building. However, the "blue plate" door openers, placed at just the right height for those in wheelchairs, are also at just the right height for a fast-moving, clever toddler, who can, in a very few seconds, make a hasty exit. The entry doors can also open unexpectedly, pinning a poorly positioned toddler against the wall.

Elevators can also present a hazard. A toddler familiar with the routine of the family entering and exiting an elevator can easily find herself traveling between floors alone, with a frantic mother left behind. Removing any of the now-standard equipment for complying with the ADA isn't the solution either. For the most part, these changes have been of benefit to all, including families. However, being aware of ways in which these conveniences can pose a problem for families is highly advisable, as professionals can become concerned observers and spotters (see "The Danger of Automatic Doors and Elevators").

Stairways

It is easy for adults to overlook the many ways in which babies are learning. In public settings such as libraries, children just learning to walk and balance are also physically learning how to navigate steps and stairways. This challenging task involves several learning activities simultaneously. The early walker is practicing gross motor movement and control. He is learning about spatial orientation and the pull of gravity and is coping with the mental challenge of taking risks. He is exercising balancing skills, gauging distance, and practicing eye-foot coordination. The early walker is also learning at the muscular level the rise of the step. This is so valuable a skill that most public buildings have specific standards and codes for how steep and wide steps and stairs must be in order for them to *be* and to *feel* safe. Even for adults, a trip up or down a nonstandard staircase can feel very awkward and unsteady.

Research shows that babies as early as sixteen months know how to use handrails. Even at this young age, babies know the difference between dependable, solid forms of support and riskier alternatives. Handrails are standard equipment in public stairways, often positioned at a few different heights. However, the height of early walkers and toddlers, arguably the largest population of precarious stair climbers, is not a consideration. They cannot comfortably reach handrails, and, even if they could, the circumference of the handrail is very large in proportion to their little hands.[1]

Furthermore, babies and toddlers learning to manage stairs can move slowly. It is courteous to be patient while patrons such as an arthritic senior citizen or a teen with a sprained knee traverse the stairs. That same consideration should be extended to toddlers and caregivers. Librarians should strive to encourage this type of physical movement and activity, as it is part of healthy development. The library can be a public place in which to practice these burgeoning skills.

Children's librarians have the unique opportunity to celebrate the littlest patrons in the public sector and to foster respect for and appreciation of their developing skills as well as their participation in the general library culture and climate, even in the stairwell.

Baby Steps

- Educate staff on how much is being learned while early walkers are using stairs, hopefully instilling a deeper respect and patience for this activity.
- Encourage parents of children in this age range to use the stairs.
- Use the staircase area for education and information, offering factoids regarding learning accomplishments, advertising library and community events, displaying art, and the like. Such materials may also placate or distract (in good ways) impatient fellow staircase users.
- Just as we have fast lanes in grocery stores, on highways, and at airports, when possible, consider the inclusion of a slow lane on wide staircases, or "slow moving traffic keep to the right" signage that makes such consideration respectful as well as whimsical, not to mention safer, for all.
- Install a small, safe play step area in the children's department so children can practice.

Big Step

- Install handrails that are at a comfortable height and diameter for the reach and grip of the average two-year-old.

Strollers

Babies and toddlers frequently visit the library in strollers, and because there is room for a wheelchair, there is also room for a stroller. However, babies and toddlers are not disabled. They are instead gaining abilities, so librarians must

The Danger of Automatic Doors and Elevators

Alice, the mother of an infant, a toddler, and a four-year-old, was at the circulation desk preparing to leave. Within a few short seconds, toddler Ian's attention was riveted on the "blue plate" handicapped-accessible automatic door opener, because the family used it all the time to enter and leave the building. Ian bolted for the plate, opened both doors, and was beyond the entryway and fully into the parking lot before his mother even noticed. A sprinting staff member who witnessed the event was right behind him, scooped him up, and safely returned him to a frantic mom. Safety and order were restored! This time. A mortified, grateful mother, never realizing the danger an automatic door could pose, sighed with relief. The moral of this story? How ironic that a device intended to do great good for the disabled could have led to tragedy, just that fast.

Young mom Angie, baby Micah, and toddler Josie had just finished their crafts after storytime and were getting ready to go home. As they awaited the elevator car, Angie and another parent struck up a conversation. Josie knew what to do! Push the button and the doors open. Go inside. Push the button and the doors close. But this time the doors opened onto a different floor! No mommy! Terror struck. The older sibling of another family saw the whole event and raced for the stairs, waiting at the next floor for Josie to arrive. Josie was then treated to another ride to be reunited with mommy. The older child was rewarded with a sweet-smelling bookmark. It really does "take a village," and that includes older children, to keep little ones safe.

keep a few caveats in mind. Babies and toddlers have about a gazillion feet of reaching distance and are incredibly fast acting. The baby riding around the library in a stroller may suddenly grab a shiny table cover and whoosh! There goes the carefully created holiday book display. Also, the turn ratio on some strollers can be somewhat wide, so librarians should be aware that some passageways may not be negotiable. And in order for children of this age to interact with the library environment, exiting the stroller will be necessary. Is there adequate inside parking? Even one stroller can take up quite a bit of space. When several caregivers, all with strollers, are having a play date in the library, considerable floor area may be consumed. For larger, spacious libraries, stroller parking may not be a problem, but for compact libraries it may pose a safety issue, especially if the strollers block regular foot traffic.

Leaving the stroller behind is an option, but there are also problems associated with being on foot. A caregiver sometimes resembles a pack mule, loaded with books, a diaper bag, device carriers, a purse, and a baby in a carrier, and, of course, holding a toddler's hand. It would be in the best interest of such a patron to not have unexpected obstacles, such as trash baskets or low tables, in main pathways.

MOVING

As discussed earlier, babies and toddlers *need* to move. Movement is one of the primary means by which they learn. Because libraries in general, and children's librarians in particular, are all about facilitating learning, providing opportunities to move about and explore is necessary. Current best practices in children's librarianship respect this need where programming is concerned. Through music, nursery rhymes, songs, and other components of baby and toddler programs, children's services providers are on top of things. However, there should also be a place in the children's area for open, free-form activity and exploration. Not all babies and toddlers are fortunate enough to be able to attend structured programs, but they are library patrons all the same. They, too, deserve to be able to interact with the library in ways specific to their abilities and limitations. This is especially the case because one of our professional goals is to foster the development of pre- and early literacy skills.

Babies in today's culture have become more limited in opportunities to move. Authorities continue to advise or to require parents to strap babies into car seats when traveling, and for good reason. Health professionals encourage parents to put babies to sleep on their backs or sides to prevent sudden infant death syndrome. And many homes do not have conditions that are suitable for tummy-time activity. Many babies spend a considerable amount of time in swings, carriers, or small, stationary play yards. Tummy-time activity is necessary for developing pre-literacy skill. It is reasonable to assume that a baby should be provided a place for this pre-reading and pre-writing activity in the library, just as it is reasonable to assume a place for wheelchair ramps and elevators.

Because babies spend so much time lying on their backs and because it is so beneficial to move about, it is in their best interest to provide a pre-literacy place they can spend time on their tummies and otherwise be unrestrained (see the feature "Freedom to Move"). A simple, enclosed mat or structure devoted to a baby's physical movement and activity does not have to be overly expensive or bulky.

When planning for baby to spend time out of the carrier, librarians should also address the caregiver's physical needs. Where will he sit while baby is free to move about? Often, although mats and other constructs are in place, there is nowhere for the adult to be comfortable other than to stand nearby and observe. Standing nearby while baby is in the play unit can be awkward and uncomfortable, thereby shortening the time an adult is willing to invest in baby's library interactivity.

In the library, the moving baby is encouraged to interact with books and other learning materials. At first, books must be brought to baby, as baby cannot obtain them independently. However, babies quickly advance from being somewhat immobile to rolling over and will make their way to objects of interest, such as a colorful board book or toy. Soon they are sitting up with assistance, then sitting alone. It then becomes much easier to manipulate and peruse the pages of a book.

Once these skills are mastered, only a few weeks pass before babies are crawling with the clear goal of retrieving a book of visual interest. Babies who are mobile need to have not only enough restrictions in place to keep them out of harm's way but also enough space to allow for adequate exercise. Ideally, the area should also include literacy-rich elements, especially books that, among other things, lure baby into movement.

As baby accomplishes independent walking, a brand new set of hazards arises. Precarious, just-learning-how-to-do-this walking implies frequent missteps, imbalances, and falls. Sharp edges and corners are known hazards in areas where babies and toddlers spend time. However, it is surprising how often children's rooms are created with little regard to this problem. Even baby board-book shelving units often have sharp, cutting edges and corners. Of course, it is unrealistic to expect the room to be totally hazard-free. Nevertheless, softened corners and edges can be used in areas where early walkers are most active.

So much physical activity is achieved in only a few short months! Because this growth happens so quickly, it is easy to dismiss the events as somehow unimportant. Babies outgrow their environments as quickly as they outgrow their shoes. Nevertheless, such spaces are crucial and well worth the investment. After all, babies come into the world every day. So just as soon as one baby is graduating from the play area, another one is ready to enter.

Libraries are beginning to include spaces in which babies can be liberated from constraints. Consider how the following suggestions could be implemented at your library.

Baby Steps

- Purchase a padded play yard suitable to your space in order to introduce the idea of babies at play in the library. It doesn't need to be excessively large in order to be effective. Optimally, it should include a mirrored surface and enough space for two or three babies, or even a caregiver. If the moderate cost is prohibitive, invite your Friends or local service group to make the purchase.
- Rearrange seating or add a chair with magazines or informational pamphlets close by for caregivers.
- Advocate for these changes in spaces and service.
- Inspect your children's room carefully, looking for sharp corners, spinning display units, and other potential hazards at the face level of an early

Freedom to Move

One area often overlooked in early literacy discussions is the value of developing gross motor control, especially in the core trunk muscles. Infant development occurs in a proximal-distal fashion, meaning that growth naturally proceeds outward, beginning in the core of the body and then moving to the developing limbs. (This process also explains why crawling happens before walking.) Babies need to spend time free to move about on their bellies as opposed to the supine state imposed by the ubiquitous, often-required car or infant seat. The reasons are numerous.[*]

First, babies are still building coordination across the brain landscape. The left and right hemispheres of the brain are still under construction, busily assimilating the synchronization of the physical body. Tummy-time exercise helps foster cohesiveness, continuity, balance, and collaboration between these two hemispheres. It also prepares the infant for the next developmental task of crawling.

Second, tummy time provides a whole-body exercise experience. By attempting to balance, reach, kick, and look up, babies' arms and legs, neck muscles, and core trunk muscles receive an intense isometric workout. Shoulders are strengthened, which leads to strong upper arms and elbows, then wrists, then hands, then, of course, fingers. Good core, gross motor muscle development in these early months is essential for the development of fine motor skills later on. Ultimately, the development of fine motor skills is required for the successful manipulation of tools, such as crayons, pencils, spoons, or screwdrivers, and for turning the pages of a book.[†]

[*] Alan Fogel, *Infancy: Infant, Family, and Society*, 4th ed. (Belmont, CA: Thompson Learning, 2001), 290–91.
[†] Therapy Center for Children, "Fine Motor Development and Handwriting," www.therapycenterfor children.com/child-fine-motor-development-handwriting-suffolk-county.php.

walker. Make attempts to remove or soften those edges and corners with inexpensive corner guards, pads, and protectors.

- Sit down on the floor in your children's room where the most active play occurs and view the scene from baby's perspective and with an eye for safety and comfort.
- Identify any cold drafts, flooring, wiring, places that might pinch or poke, and so on that could present a hazard.
- Rearrange furnishings, make suitable repairs, and purchase simple outlet covers.
- Relocate play to another corner of the room, as necessary.
- Appropriately decorate walls and other surfaces with baby's visual field in mind, even at the checkout stations.

Big Steps

- Install a permanent soft space for babies so they can safely be freed from their constraint seats to interact with the environment. Within the space, babies should be able to reach their own book collection, interact with other babies, and spend some valuable tummy time.
- Reroute heat flow in the baby play area to address cold drafts low to the ground.

HELPING EVERYONE TAKE A SEAT

Librarians have many things to consider when making seating purchases for babies and care providers. For example, beanbag chairs are a fun seating option. They are squishy and portable. Little children love them, as do teens. However, they can generate a few concerns. If they are broken open, the contents pose a choking hazard. If randomly relocated, they could present a tripping hazard. Soft, overstuffed chairs can also pose a problem because they can be difficult for senior caregivers or very pregnant mommies to manage. Sometimes seating may be too comfortable, perhaps inviting patrons who otherwise do not belong in the children's area. Chairs that are cloth-covered are more difficult to keep clean and stain-free. (They can also harbor tiny, unwanted guests such as bedbugs, fleas, and lice.) Finally, many chairs in children's areas are modeled after adult seating options. Inevitably, they are very tip-able, and a newly walking and climbing little one can easily upset such a chair, spilling its contents loudly and perhaps painfully.

Café-style seating has a few advantages that are unique to children's areas. The seat itself is more at hip level, making it easier to simply perch as opposed to fully sit, allowing for quick response time should a child need immediate attention. Also, because the seat is higher, the vantage point makes a quick overview of the room a bit easier. Pregnant women and older patrons frequently prefer these chairs because they are easier to exit. This style of seating invites a more casual and friendly atmosphere. Finally, café tables and seats are usually smaller in circumference than a standard round library table, and they can either be permanently installed or remain portable, depending on the library's particular needs.

Glider rockers are also an option, provided that they are constructed in such a way as to cover any mechanisms that may pose a pinching hazard. These chairs can also be found with extra-wide seats, covered with washable vinyl, that will accommodate both an adult and a small child, or a person of considerable girth. Although very comfortable, glider rockers take up quite a bit of space, are rather expensive, and aren't necessarily constructed to withstand hard use. Still, they are very much appreciated by nursing mothers.

To provide adequate seating in limited spaces for a wide range of sizes and ages is indeed challenging. Seating should be comfortable yet firm and easy to exit. Arthritic grandparents, individuals with disabilities, those of large girth, and very pregnant women all need to be considered along with early walkers and preschoolers. Further, all seating should be solid, attractive, and easy to clean. The options for seating, upholstery, and utility have changed tremendously since the early days of traditional furnishings for the children's section of the library. Adult chairs built in smaller sizes aren't (and never really have been) quite adequate. However, today's library design teams are beginning to assess these issues, and, as a result, it is easier than ever before to rise to the challenge of making the children's area, especially the little corner for babies and care-givers, a suitably furnished one.

Seating options have expanded greatly in the past several years. Become more familiar with them, such as toddler chairs that cannot tip, soft-surface seating that does not harbor unwanted "guests," and heavier duty, extra-wide, straight-backed styles.

Baby Steps

- Study the area, watching for such occurrences as standing-room only, standing as the only alternative, or standing for fear of not being able to exit existing seating without embarrassment.
- Take a real or virtual field trip to assess your options. For example, tod-dler chairs that cannot tip are now more readily available.
- Purchase a few unique items as prototypes, being especially attentive to safety, utility, and cost.

Big Steps

- Replace current seating altogether, paying particular attention to how existing seating is being used (and not used).
- Invite interior design professionals (as well as students) who specialize in preschool structures to offer their solutions. Include those who special-ize in engineering seating and other furnishings that may be of value to families with special needs.

USING ELECTRONIC DEVICES SAFELY

Providing safe spaces in the library is a must, as all would agree. However, babies in the library present rather unique safety issues when the adult wants to use a computer. Typically, the library's computer workstations are housed in the adult services area. Of course, we all know that this arrangement is not optimal for any baby and adult, but it is common. Out of necessity, the baby carrier, baby included, is parked on the floor, creating a tripping hazard for anyone walking by. It is obviously unsafe for the baby. The adult, innocently enough, does not have the baby in his immediate visual field and may become absorbed in whatever task is at hand, not noticing potential dangers. Toddlers in this situation can quickly become a nuisance to others or simply wander off. As far as space planning is concerned, this situation isn't very respectful of the needs of all involved. Staff members have to monitor these areas and address complaints and concerns. Other patrons become annoyed or irritated, or they simply cannot concentrate. Parents or caregivers as legitimate library technology users are placed in an awkward situation, and fussy babies become innocent yet unwelcome intruders.

The situation becomes even more complicated when the toddler sibling is added to the mix. What is she going to do while the adult is attending to his computer tasks? Are siblings left unattended in the children's department while the adult and baby are on the opposite side of the building? Or do the children remain in the adult area where their presence can pose problems? All these scenarios are not optimal for anyone, including librarians and support staff.

For the most part, parents want to be able to have their children within view and still be able to attend to their own computer-related tasks. They would prefer to not annoy others or cause problems. Some parents and caregivers have no alternative but to use the library for necessary computer-related tasks. However, Internet use policies and hardware placements are not always family-friendly. Further, technology centers for adults usually do not allow concurrent learning for infants, toddlers, and other children.

As the world of technology evolves, it continues to produce a dizzying array of devices that are carried about in the pocket, purse, and diaper bag. Free access to the Internet is one of the primary reasons why these devices are carted to the library, accompanied by cords, chargers, cases, and bags (see the feature "Electrical Outlets, Devices, and Babies"). In an ideal library setting, workstations with battery-charging capabilities should be located within the children's play area (with cords and plugs safely tucked away). Not only are "dead devices" highly inconvenient, they may be detrimental when the parent is awaiting a call from a physician, a pharmacy, or an older child. The well-planned children's area should include such charging stations. Perhaps in a perfect world the adult caregiver could just leave the technology aside for a while and enjoy playing with

Electrical Outlets, Devices, and Babies

Dan approached the children's desk and asked if there was an electrical outlet somewhere in which he could recharge his laptop. His wife was home battling the flu, and he was trying to provide her with some much-needed rest. His one-year-old daughter, Zoe, was contentedly playing in the children's area, where he was hoping to accomplish a few necessary computer-related tasks. He needed to plug in his computer, but the only outlets available were the type that are installed in the floor like small manhole covers embedded in the carpet. As is usual for parents, he made do by positioning his chair over the now-exposed, open outlet to keep his daughter somewhat shielded. Their visit passed without incident. Nevertheless, there it was—an open outlet in the middle of the room at toddler and crawler access range, wires as a tripping hazard, and a general public area that was not designed with necessity, convenience, or children's safety in mind. Of course, Dan could have just hauled his one-year-old over to the adult area where, in this particular library, plug-in stations are plentiful but play is frowned upon.

her little one. However, anyone respecting the fast-flowing, techno-cultural changing tide knows that this approach is just not realistic.

Be intentional yet realistic about providing safe spaces for babies and their siblings and care providers, keeping technology needs in mind, at the same time and in the same place. These areas should be gently corralling and include good sight lines for the adults. Such an area not only makes it easier for care providers to keep an eye on their children but also places the responsibility of monitoring their children squarely on their shoulders, thus relieving the library staff of any assumption to the contrary.

Baby Steps

- Install an adult-use computer for care providers in the children's area in a relatively out-of-the-way place so that baby can be nearby and out of harm's way and older siblings are within the adult's visual field.
- Reacquaint library staff with building policies regarding unattended children, especially those of adults who are immersed in their virtual worlds.
- Invite local children's services providers or other professionals to educate or update staff members on the impact of technology trends and legal issues relative to families of babies and young children.
- Whenever possible, enclose or hide exposed electrical and electronic cords and wires.

Big Steps

- Design and construct computer workstations that provide ample space for placing the baby on the desktop, or even on a tabletop, instead of on the drafty floor.
- Completely overhaul the children's area using the suggestions and models described in this chapter.
- Provide laptop computers for in-house-only checkout so that a parent can attend to computer-related tasks while remaining in the play area.
- Carefully determine placement of technology when planning new children's spaces, making electrical outlets available to adults yet in safe ways.
- Have an electrical contractor evaluate and, if necessary, reroute existing outlets to provide safe access in order to meet care providers' electricity and technology needs.

FEEDING AND NURSING

Babies get hungry, of course, and their hunger cry is one of the most uncomfortable sounds to strike the human ear. The pressure a parent can feel in a public building under such circumstances is enormous. Escaping the situation, however, doesn't necessarily mean exiting the building, although for some that may appear to be the only alternative. Simply providing seating "around the corner" or slightly screened can make for a happier library visit for all.

Creating a comfortable nursing station that is family-friendly clearly sends a message of welcome and respect for babies and their mommies and other care providers. It also removes the likelihood of offending other, more conservative patrons, thus respecting their sensibilities as well.

Babies, especially as they get to nine and ten months, can be hefty. Nursing a twenty-pound infant for ten to fifteen minutes can produce great strain on a mother's arms and back. When purchasing furniture for this area, keep in mind the need for support of the arms and back for the nursing or bottle-feeding caregiver.

Babies and toddlers up to about two years old are working and thinking very hard. Therefore, they may get hungry, tired, and cranky, sometimes quite suddenly! Many libraries are becoming more relaxed in their policies regarding food and drink. Although permitting such activity may be counter to some libraries' policies, perhaps leniency can be offered for babies and toddlers, with a small area set aside to allow the consumption of dry snacks.

Baby Steps

- Evaluate your existing furniture floor plan with respect to the needs of a nursing mother.
- Provide pre-literacy entertainment and enrichment in this area for toddler siblings, such as self-contained, magnet-style tracing boards, manipulative toys, coloring activities, puppets, and simple puzzles.
- Revisit existing policies regarding food in the library. If possible, make concessions for babies and toddlers, and their anxious caregivers, that allow simple snacks.
- Use this seating and feeding situation as a teaching opportunity with a captive audience by posting messages and early learning tips, sharing local news and information, providing parenting periodicals, and the like in the vicinity.
- Provide hand sanitizer and wipes.
- Keep a small, handheld vacuum nearby for quick cleanup.

Big Steps

- Purchase comfortable glider rockers that are mother-, infant-, and toddler-friendly.
- Include a slightly tucked-away area for nursing when making major renovations.

DIAPERING AND ALL THINGS RESTROOM

While I was researching and interviewing families for this book, the topic of public restrooms elicited by far the most outspoken responses from parents, caregivers, and frustrated children's librarians! They were only too eager to get some things off their chests regarding public restrooms and the overall sociocultural lack of respect for the needs of little children and their care providers (see the feature "Families in the Public Restroom"). Although many public restrooms are better than they used to be, so much more needs to be considered, and children's librarians must be included in the planning of these spaces.

One of the most basic and immediate needs of all babies is a diaper change. As cute and sweet as babies can be, they can also present a less attractive side. It's very smelly and unpleasant, and typically they don't like it any more than anyone else does. And the resultant crying isn't really wanted either. In planning public

Families in the Public Restroom

S teve and his little daughter, Gracie, in the same restroom? Already, as he reports it, "high on everyone's radar," this single father of a little girl is very cautious and self-conscious. Gracie is just learning to use the bathroom. Should Steve take his daughter to the men's room or the ladies' room? Both situations are not comfortable. If there are no "family" facilities, what are his options but to "choose wrongly" or just not visit the library?

Mindy, with four small children, says, "I just plan a fast pick-up and delivery visit, thus avoiding the whole 'potty' thing. My children don't very often come into the library."

Ten-month-old Liam is a wiggly little boy. He is still trying to master the balance necessary to sit up alone. Mom has to use the bathroom. She reports that the jump seat in the handicapped stall could be very helpful for holding Liam in place, if it wasn't six feet away from her reach! With a bit of an embarrassed smile, mom says that her timing must be impeccable.

Amanda has two daughters, a ten-month-old and a two-year-old, and she has to go to the bathroom. Restroom visits, according to Amanda, are "so not pretty! I have the baby in a football hold and try to keep the two-year-old distracted so she doesn't touch anything!"

spaces, designers often neglect to factor in a place for adults to address this issue. Parents are left with few options—leave the library even though they just arrived, try to change the baby in an unaccommodating public restroom, or try to sneak in a change back in the stacks somewhere. None of these scenarios is optimal, not to mention baby-friendly. However, it may surprise some administrators to learn how often such events occur. Thankfully, baby-changing stations in public settings are becoming more commonplace. But this solution is only a partial one.

In just a few short months, once-immobile babies are crawling, walking, curious, and *very* mobile. Being turned loose in a public restroom can lead to some generally unhealthy exploration. Who would willingly put a ten-month-old early walker in such a situation? Well, mom needs to go potty, too. Or perhaps mom needs to change the diaper of her three-month-old. What is she going to do with the baby's two-year-old sibling? It would be difficult to fully accept babies in the library without anticipating such situations and doing all we can to make their visit a little, maybe even a *lot*, easier.

As a rule, public buildings require that strollers, carts, and the like remain parked outside restrooms, and rightfully so. And, of course, we do not want unattended children—ever. So the whole family leaves carriers, carts, and strollers and enters the restroom. Once inside, the family encounters more challenges. Is a child-sized toilet available? Can a two- to three-year-old reach the toilet paper? Potty training, after all, comes with the family package.

Hand washing should also be possible without the adult having to hold the toddler off the floor while struggling with the water and soap. One alternative is to just skip the hand washing altogether, which, of course, is not an optimal alternative. And, if there is an automatic hand dryer, likely it is positioned so that it blasts the toddler in the face. Air dryers can also be painfully loud, hot, and downright frightening! Paper towels do so much more than dry hands. They also mop up tears and sweat and blot spills. Even if the library has a no-paper-towel policy, perhaps exceptions can be made in the family restroom.

A dry shelf or a few hooks should be available so an adult can dig through a bag for necessities without the bag becoming saturated on a wet countertop. Early walkers and toddlers should be able to reach the top of the trash receptacle. And a toddler-sized, strap-down jump seat available *within adult reach* while the adult attends to "business" is highly appreciated.

These relatively simple fixes can speak volumes of acceptance to parents of young children, especially to those who are new to bringing babies and their toddler siblings into a public library setting. One mother exclaimed, "Who is responsible for designing these bathrooms, anyway? Obviously not anyone who has kids!" Another stated, "We, as mothers, just deal with it. It's just what we are expected to do." A father of three children who was also a library director reported his frustration with a design team that wanted to put the family restroom on another floor and down the hall from the children's area. He could *not* get the architects to understand that when a child is potty training, there is no time for making it "down the stairs, then down the hall." He had to argue the point to finally get the family restroom located near the children's department . . . and he was the director!

As a public institution that intentionally invites babies, toddlers, and families, the library is obliged to make those visits as comfortable as possible. Libraries taking respectful, proactive steps to provide family-friendly restroom facilities have the potential to model quality restroom planning not only for other libraries but for all institutions and places of commerce that invite this population.

Baby Steps

- If your library has not already done so, install baby-changing stations in both the men's and the women's restrooms.
- Install at least one constraining jump seat in the restroom for early walkers, positioned within reach of the adult toilet.

- Provide hooks both within and outside stalls on which to hang purses, diaper bags, laptop carriers, or coats.
- Provide a shelf or other flat surface for bags and purses away from the sink area.
- In unusual cases, offer to "police the door" for parents and children of opposite genders, as necessary.
- Make sure toddlers and preschoolers can reach the toilet paper.
- Provide a step stool to help little ones reach the sink.
- Invite administrators to a discussion about these issues, challenges, and concerns.
- Ask to be included on design committees. Ask again.
- Ask care providers for further suggestions.

Big Steps

- Whenever possible, install child-sized toilets that don't self-flush, because an unexpected flush can truly terrify a little one.
- Survey adults with young children for their ideas regarding comfortable, welcoming restrooms designed for the whole family package.
- When planning remodels or updating existing libraries, create family-friendly restrooms near the children's area with the preceding suggestions in mind.

CREATING A SAFE, FAMILY-FRIENDLY LIBRARY

Experiencing the library from the point of view of the care provider is a wonderful way to better understand this patron's underlying needs. For parents and caregivers, the visit begins long before they arrive, as they endure the car seats, traffic, snacks, parking lots, crying jags, doorways and entrances, carpets and tile, echoes and muffles, elevators and stairs, equipment and supplies, conversations and interruptions. These families are to be applauded for even making the effort!

Baby Steps

- Install hooks at varying heights to accommodate a variety of accoutrements such as book bags, diaper bags, coats, oversized blankets, backpacks, lanyards, and even some types of toys, thus keeping clutter off the floor as much as possible. Avoid hangers because small children cannot manage them and older children generally ignore them.

- Visit an unfamiliar library. If possible, take a baby and a toddler with you, perhaps even using a two-seat stroller.
- Provide staff training about the importance of accepting families in the library and acknowledge staff members' patience and compassion.
- With permission of course, shadow a young family going to the library. Start at their driveway. Browse the children's area from their perspective.
- Visit other libraries in your vicinity. Create a checklist indicating such things as the quality of personal service, levels of acceptance, restroom accommodations, and availability of books within infant and toddler reach.
- If there are several staff members in the children's department, include them in your field trip. Choose a variety of libraries.
- Spend some time discussing challenges of service to this population with children's librarians in other locations and listen for their creative solutions for your own library.
- Brainstorm ways in which the library can alter its public image regarding babies in the library. Although excluding babies is outmoded in most libraries, outside the library the stereotype persists.

Big Steps

- When opportunities arise that include reallocating space in the library, pay particular attention to some of the issues identified in this chapter and make them priorities in the design.
- Invite children's librarians to building and remodeling planning sessions, respecting their input as child development specialists and advocates for this population.
- Include parents and other professionals who work with families of young children outside the field of librarianship in these design sessions.
- Seek grant-writing opportunities to underwrite both major and minor projects.

ATTENDING TO PHYSICAL NEEDS

Making even minor changes to existing spaces speaks respectfully to the needs of families with babies and toddlers. These changes alone make the very important proclamation that all family members should be in the library together. This isn't a new idea. Virginia Walter, at the end of the last century, asserted that "[q]uality service for infants and toddlers even requires rethinking the physical environment in many libraries."[2] Within carefully appointed spaces, along with the librarian, families have the opportunity to engage in activities that make lasting, brain-building, positive impacts. Families can experience a place of their very own and are free (and freed up!) to engage in play that further fosters healthy development.

Librarians are actively making great strides in the right direction when it comes to creating appropriate spaces and making adequate physical provisions for babies and families. They also offer baby-friendly programs, books, and toys as well as library-appropriate, literacy-based play. However, libraries still need to create cohesive spaces and general service packages that better suit the needs of this population in *one* area, *concurrently.*

Many families are missing out on this rich and rewarding experience, unaware of the programs and collections designed expressly for babies and toddlers, bogged down by outdated stereotypes that have historically sent an unwelcoming message. A great move in the right direction is to consider how basic physical changes can be made in the local public library so that the message is clear: families with babies and toddlers are welcome and wanted. For some families, the first step in becoming lifelong library users is to stroll through the door—and feel good about doing so.

Notes

1. Sarah E. Berger and Karen E. Adolph, "Infants Use Handrails as Tools in a Locomotor Task," *Developmental Psychology* 39, no. 3 (2003): 594–605; Sarah E. Berger, Karen E. Adolph, and Sharon A. Lobo, "Out of the Toolbox: Toddlers Differentiate Wobbly and Wooden Handrails," *Child Development* (November–December 2005): 1294–307.

2. Virginia A. Walter, *Children and Libraries: Getting It Right* (Chicago: American Library Association, 2001), 87.

EMOTIONAL EXPRESSIONS

The Unfolding Emotional Lives of Families

NYONE OCCUPYING THE PUBLIC LIBRARY BRINGS ALONG his emotional self. Library patrons as well as staff members may be experiencing a variety of emotions on any given day, including sadness, elation, depression, broken-heartedness, silliness, and loneliness. Emotions are felt by everyone, sometimes in simultaneous and conflicting combinations. The human emotional landscape is vast and baffling, deeply personal, and as unique as a fingerprint in its manifestations or expressions.

Like adults, babies and toddlers have emotional lives. Unlike adults, who (usually) can identify their current mood or state, little ones experience emotional lives that are still under construction and much more volatile, surprising, mysterious, and sometimes overwhelming. For example, the twelve-month-old may be happily immersed in play and in the next minute be kicking and clawing in a fit of frustration, and in the next, distracted and calm. It will take a long time, a lot of patience, and much practice for the growing child, from birth all the way through young adulthood, to come to terms with her developing emotional life. This process is also impacted by the unique experiences and temperament of the child and unfolds in the presence of the traits and experiences of the family into which she is born. Too, the library itself, as a living institution with its various staff members who also have affecting personalities, contains an emotional component that varies from day to day. Together, these elements factor into the everyday event of a family visit to the library.

EMOTIONAL GROWTH: THE DEVELOPMENTAL TIME LINE

As with all other components of the first few months of an infant's life, much is being accomplished within his emotional landscape. From birth, he is able to express a variety of emotions, such as interest, distress, and disgust. He can also display contentment in his quiet moments. By two months he will be capable of expressing a wider variety of emotions, such as delight, confusion, frustration, uncertainty, bewilderment, perplexity, and shyness. Before the fourth month of life, he will have learned to "read" others' faces and will be able to mirror in his facial expressions their emotions, such as sadness, happiness, and surprise. (In a way, he is practicing an early form of "reading," using symbols, clues, and cues in context, similar to acquiring print reading skills!) Even at this early stage, he is able to match the adult's facial expression to the tone of voice—he will become quite confused if he hears a sad tone of voice while the adult displays a smiling face. And so, from birth, he is learning the language needed to label his feelings. He is building the "emotions" vocabulary that he will, some day, use to communicate his feelings verbally.

By four months, the once-contented and friendly baby begins to recognize that some people are familiar and can be trusted and that others are unknowns. Using a series of behaviors, called *stranger anxiety* by researchers, baby may now begin to shy away from, avoid, or otherwise negatively respond to those less familiar. If the librarian has been fortunate enough to have seen the baby and had the opportunity to interact frequently, exchanges at this stage may be unremarkable. But if baby is not familiar with the librarian, it is likely that he will resist or become anxious. Regardless of the behavior exhibited, the librarian shouldn't feel discouraged if baby displays any negativity or avoidance because this reaction is normal.

Baby will also display intense frustration as he attempts to reach a toy, move about, or otherwise problem solve. It is tempting to want to assist baby, but a healthy amount of frustration is a good thing, as it motivates him to accomplish his goals. When he masters those goals, his joy is infectious, and he and his observers delight in the accomplishment!

By eight months, baby will begin to indicate feelings of joy and affection for his primary care providers. He has learned to trust them and looks to them for clues about how to respond to events, such as meeting new babies, being presented with an object, or entering a strange room. He is also becoming more mobile and exploratory and, therefore, more wary of activity in the area. At this stage, feelings of vulnerability can quickly turn to frightful tears should his care provider "disappear" behind a bookshelf or a newspaper. All play and learning cease until baby is once again reassured that all is well.

As baby grows into toddlerhood, he becomes more comfortable with his surroundings. Gradually, his earlier anxieties begin to lessen, and he will begin to risk interacting with others. This opens up new challenges as he learns to navigate the larger world of other people's emotions. Baby will begin to use words to express feelings and can even connect facial symbols to words and delight in simple games, such as "Show me your silly face." Baby moves gently into a fuller sense of self and individuality, learning at around eighteen months that the reflection he sees in the mirror is none other than himself. Researchers believe that consciousness becomes part of the child's lived experience as a result of this facial recognition. Emotions such as self-consciousness, guilt, shame, pride, deprecation, esteem, self-worth, and embarrassment are now more fully experienced. (Although put-downs, deprecations, insults, and the like may be lost on little children, their fragile emotional selves still can read the adult's tone of voice and facial expressions, thereby experiencing negative feelings.)

Baby has fully grown into toddlerhood when he learns the meaning of, and how to employ, the word "no." One of the most powerful words in the English language, this little word allows for the expression of independence. It also serves as a tool for adults to set limits and provide safety for their now-mobile walkers. And toddlers hear it all day long in such frustrating statements as "No, get off the table," "No, don't play with your milk," "No, you may not have another cookie." "No" is also pressed into service by the child as he discovers that he, too, has an opinion—and the ability to express it. It is the word that communicates willfulness, or unwillingness, and allows for the expression of individuality, personal preferences, likes, dislikes, and differences of opinion. As a result, it can be the source of heated exchanges. Young children practicing the word "no" won't necessarily mean it either. "Would you like a cracker?" asks dad. "No," says toddler, while happily receiving the verbally refused treat. It is a perfectly acceptable answer that we are sometimes taken aback in hearing. A simple question such as "Do you want to play with the doll?" may elicit this surprising answer. However, no means no. The toddler is simply practicing the right to assert his own opinion. And, of course, that opinion could change very quickly—or not!

ENCOURAGING HEALTHY EMOTIONAL GROWTH

Emotional influences occur in contextual situations, such as a first meeting, a surprising event, a new toy, or a solitary playful activity. They are also caught up with other senses. Just the smell of new books or white glue can evoke long-forgotten feelings in adults. The implication for librarians is that library encounters are full of emotionally impacting potential, for both good and maybe not so good. Babies' brains are still in the process of making neuronal connections that will be couched with the emotions they are experiencing. We sometimes notice this phenomenon as adults when we revisit a place from our past, such as a childhood school or playground, and feelings surface that we may not have experienced in years. This reminder of how deeply affecting the library experience can be for a child underscores the importance of creating library experiences that are positive ones. Of course, librarians and support staff alike should strive to make the library a happy place where happy experiences can be anticipated and enjoyed.

Young children are working hard to understand and master their intense feelings. Because they cannot yet articulate those feelings, they may act out in more physical ways, such as biting, hitting, pushing, hugging, grabbing, jumping, squealing, or pouting. Further, children dealing with stressors such as the inclusion of a new sibling, a change in family dynamics, or a relocation may exhibit behaviors that they have long since outgrown, such as reverting to thumb sucking, demanding a bottle, wanting to be carried, and so on. In effect, they are using behaviors that, in the past, brought some form of comfort and feeling of security.

Inviting babies into healthy, "feel-good" experiences at the library is an opportunity to build positive neuronal connections to library places. Happy and engaging interactions with the librarian reinforce and strengthen those emotional ties deep within the baby's developing brain.

Baby Steps

- Smile and talk with babies so that your familiarity with them in your library is a warm, soothing emotional encounter.
- Mirror baby's unhappy facial expression to show your empathy. Then change your expression to a happy one. Sometimes the baby will follow your lead and smile back!
- Become more informed about the emotional development of babies and young children. YouTube offers a wealth of vignettes on this topic. (Search key words "YouTube and babies and emotions and research" for many options!)
- Watch the YouTube vignettes with the sound off, paying particular attention to children's facial expressions in order to better identify what their expressions are telling you.
- Share what you learn and brainstorm implications for the interactions among caregiver, child, and librarian.
- Invite early childhood professionals from the community to staff meetings to discuss trends in healthy and unhealthy emotional development.

Big Steps

- Invite professionals at the academic level who specialize in infant and early childhood development to create workshops and seminars that focus attention on this topic, both in-house and at larger collaborative convention events.
- Attend a class or workshop outside the library profession related to this topic. Consult with your local job and family services departments for suggestions.

NURTURING EMOTIONAL EXPRESSIONS

Generally speaking, children are emotion-driven. Their brains have not yet matured enough to both understand and regulate their emotions, and children will continue to deal with this issue well into puberty. Impulsive outbreaks can happen as babies and toddlers learn to identify and manage strong emotions such as anger, exuberance, excitement, frustration, anxiety, and jealousy. Very young children can become swamped by the enormity of their emotional responses. Overreactive emotional hijacking can come at any time, and as a surprise to both the child and the adult. For example, what started out for the toddler as a crying response to being told that it is time to put the toys away turns into heaving sobs and wails. The response exceeds the cause and cannot easily be brought back under control, much to the discomfort of the adult.[1]

Blossoming Trust

Eighteen-month-old Sarah and her mommy have been coming to the library ever since Sarah was an infant. Every week, Sarah has been invited to have her hand stamped with a picture of a princess, a balloon, or whatever other stamp the librarian is using for that day. Mommy, however, has been receiving the stamp as timid, fearful Sarah turns away from the librarian. On one of their latest visits, Sarah, now walking, toddles up to the low desktop and, of her own volition, extends her hand "way up there" toward the librarian. The librarian, intuiting the message, gently places a stamp on Sarah's little hand. Newly developed trust has been achieved, shyness and fear overcome, and friendship between Sarah and her librarian has been established. The librarian can now feel more confident in serving Sarah directly without eliciting a fear response, and the two of them can move forward with Sarah knowing that her librarian respects her feelings.

The library visit presents a wonderful opportunity to experience positive emotions and practice self-expression in a safe, neutral environment. As members of this population begin to interact in these early social settings, they often have first-time opportunities to encounter and then process the feelings that accompany such events as taking turns, waiting, and sharing. Over time, positive library visits carry the potential of creating brains that are foundationally constructed to perceive the library as a happy, comfortable place (see the feature "Blossoming Trust"). Finally, should a toddler pitch a major tantrum when it is time to go, consider it a compliment to the great job the library is doing in making her feel welcome and in providing her with positive experiences, so much so that she doesn't want to leave.

Older, preschool- and grade-school-age children can, and should be expected to, conduct library business and interactions with a certain level of emotional self-control, sophistication, and maturity. However, the developing little ones cannot be expected to master appropriate library behaviors unless they have the opportunity to learn and then practice the skills necessary to achieve those behaviors. If librarians wish to provide a welcoming atmosphere for babies and toddlers, then they should expect emotional outbreaks. Squeals of delight, outspoken "No!"s, and cries of disappointment or frustration are going to happen and simply need to be accepted, tolerated, and seen for what they are. Not only are these emotional expressions developmentally appropriate, they are being exercised and (it is hoped) eventually mastered in the neutral, accepting environment of the public library.

Everyday encounters offer many opportunities to build deep emotional connections. There's no need to try too hard. Sometimes just a simple distraction, such as pointing to an interesting picture or singing a few bars, is enough to rein in the situation.

Baby Steps

- Try not to make a big deal out of toddler outbursts, as they are normal.
- Name the emotion you are witnessing, building a vocabulary base for the toddler and future preschooler to use. Be specific, using more nuanced words such as *frustrated, intimidated,* and *ecstatic,* when appropriate.
- *Respect* baby and toddler feelings and emotions. Even when emotional expressions are inappropriate for the situation or are a source of irritation, babies' and toddlers' feelings are real to them in the moment.
- Try not to allow your own feelings to be hurt or in other ways be offended when an infant or toddler expresses negativity aimed at you, remembering that babies and toddlers are striving to develop in this area.

- Actively seek out and purchase board books, simple nonfiction books, and media materials that help to identify and name various emotions.
- Post labeled pictures of babies displaying a variety of facial expressions.

Big Steps

- Conduct a survey that will help to assess the emotional climate of the library in general and the children's department in particular. Discuss the findings, not only among children's staff but also with administration and support staff.
- Create a strategic plan to further enhance positive feelings and to alter negative perceptions.
- Offer seminars at staff development events that address dealing with different temperaments in healthy ways, both among staff members and with regard to the public. (This suggestion might be welcome for all library clientele, not just families with young children.)

HANDLING TANTRUMS WITH TACTFUL TOLERANCE

In optimal development, babies are bonding with their primary care providers. This attachment is achieved through daily interactions with care providers and their responses to babies' expressions of need. These expressions primarily take the form of crying. Therefore, it is impossible to "spoil" an infant, as responding quickly to these cries is required for the development of healthy attachment and the building of trust between infant and caregiver. Some parents, especially first-time parents, are still learning the different nuances of baby's cries (see the feature "Temperament"). As parents become more experienced with the cries of their baby, they become better at fulfilling the need and alleviating the disruptive situation.

Most certainly, a parent or caregiver cannot control whether and when a child will cry. These adults may interpret a noisy, unpredictable crying event as unacceptable in the library. For library staff to reveal an increased level of intolerance or unwelcome, even innocently, creates an impossible situation. The expectation is just not realistic, placing both care provider and baby in unfair circumstances. In addition, a new mom may not always trust her uncertain, new-parent skill set to be able to deliver a quick solution to relieve baby's cries, should such a (likely) event happen. Even an experienced caregiver cannot guarantee complete success in quickly stopping an infant's or toddler's emotional outbursts or cries of distress.

Temperament

B abies come into the world packaged with a particular temperament. *Temperament* is defined as "the stable behavioral and emotional reactions that appear early and are influenced in part by genetic constitution."* Psychologists identify three general categories of temperament: difficult (irritable, fussy, easily upset), easy (relaxed, adaptable, friendly), and slow to warm up (cautious, tentative, a bit shy). Even at birth, babies will exhibit these basic personality traits. This simply means that some babies, just because of their general temperament, will cry more than others.

Of course, crying is the primary means by which a baby communicates. However, a crying baby is very difficult for everyone to tolerate. Some researchers believe that an infant's cry is one of the most painful, challenging sounds to strike the human ear, eliciting the edgy need to "do something" to make it stop.† Who hasn't had a run-in with a crying child in a restaurant or airplane, causing general discomfort for everyone within earshot, and a collective sigh of relief when the crying ceases (or leaves)? This is one of the reasons that libraries, with their reputation for expecting quiet, come fully against the reality for care providers and their babies.

---

* Jerome Kagan, *Galen's Prophecy: Temperament and Human Nature* (New York: Basic Books, 1995), 40.
† Alok Jha, "Why Crying Babies Are So Hard to Ignore," *Neuroscience* (October 2012), www.theguardian.com/science/2012/oct/17/crying-babies-hard-ignore.

Not only crying can present a problem. Even the happy outburst can provoke anxiety for the adult. Babies and young children may erupt in squeals of delight. They may shout out for a parent, burst into song, or squeal over a bug. These charming displays elicit feelings of delight and amusement for the caregiver, as they should. The librarian serving this population would, of course, share in those feelings of enjoyment, right? However, the adult in such circumstances may need reassurance to alleviate any guilt he may feel, thinking that such outbursts should be curtailed and controlled (see the feature "Professional Adherence to [In]tolerance").

The solution to noisy emotional occurrences in the library is rather simple: allow and validate them. Babies are going to cry, and that isn't going to change. The new parent's or uncertain caregiver's ability to end the crying may require some fumbling and false starts. At the very least, success cannot be guaranteed. That, too, isn't going to change. Toddlers will have outbursts as they learn about, enjoy, and explore their library, as should be expected. What *can* change is the library's expectation and reputation of requiring "quiet" in areas that serve families with young children. Libraries across the country are making great strides in lowering their expectation of quiet in the library. However, perceptions outside the library persist. Many adults still believe that unpredictable babies and toddlers cannot be safely trusted to be quiet in the library and therefore have no business there. This perception can, and most certainly needs, to change.

Those working within the profession know that the culture of quiet is no longer relevant. But those outside the library world, particularly nonusers with infants and toddlers, may not be aware of these changes. Discuss the situation with administration and staff. Eliciting suggestions, concerns, observations, and library culture with respect to this issue are all steps in the right direction. Brainstorm solutions within the local environment. Any approach that is respectful to the feelings of the child also serves to lessen any discomfort or embarrassment experienced by the adult.

Professional Adherence to (In)tolerance

Librarians who work with children are, without doubt, a very committed group. They are drawn to the profession because they truly care about the children in the communities they serve. They are well aware of what it means to serve the public, with all its various issues, and often feel overwhelming compassion for the children. Their workday generally enjoys delightful exchanges and experiences. In serving this population, librarians encourage repeat visits, paving the way for greater familiarity and relationship building. These are wonderful encounters that hold tremendous potential for good for everyone involved. However, sometimes bigger issues present themselves.

Children's librarians encounter such sticky situations as name-calling, shouting, put-downs, and passive neglect as well as inappropriate, ineffective, or excessive disciplinary methods. These circumstances can be even more grievous when infants and toddlers are involved. It is the hope and desire of children's librarians to attract *every* child to the library, along with their care providers. However, as most librarians have experienced, sometimes the interchanges between family members and little children border on the inappropriate or dysfunctional. These problems are generally acknowledged within the profession but rarely discussed in the wider professional literature.

It decidedly falls outside the range of library services to babies and toddlers and other children to become involved in these family issues. However, it is well within the parameters of the profession to make referrals to agencies that may be able to intervene and to report to the proper authorities any suspicions or concerns.

If the librarian should *ever* suspect that the child or even the adult is somehow in harm's way, it is quite within the profession's range of responsibility to refer the situation to appropriate authorities. Furthermore, authorities advise that anyone working in the field of children's services should err on the side of caution and, without hesitation or apology, make those reports. If the librarian feels uncomfortable with any of these awkward situations, she should refer them to appropriate administrators.

Baby Steps

- Reroute traffic patterns so that families can navigate toward their "safe zone" quickly and comfortably.
- Rearrange play sections and seating so that families can congregate in somewhat separate, contained areas.
- Create a catchphrase or simple song that can be used as a slogan or chant whenever little ones become overly rambunctious (for example, "In the library we use walking feet, inside voices, and gentle play"), keeping things positive and emphasizing what little ones *can* do.
- Avoid using scolding "don't" phrases (for example, "Don't run"). Such phrases deliver a negative message and tone.
- Deliver any admonishments deemed necessary with a positive, smiling delivery (for example, "We play quietly in the library") so as to protect fragile egos.
- Take advantage of teachable moments to educate patrons on appropriate behavior in the library, doing so in pleasant ways.
- Purchase or create an inexpensive, special, unique-to-this-purpose award sticker, bookmark, or other simple gift or reward for "best behavior" for more challenging behavior cases.
- Create special, welcome-baby brochures for inclusion in hospital bags that are offered to new mothers, indicating the changes in libraries regarding noise level.
- Disseminate child-friendly promotional brochures through local daycare centers, preschools, home-school families, pediatricians' offices, and other places that young families typically visit.
- Use social media to highlight programs, interactions, and spontaneous activities in the library, demonstrating the acceptable level of noise and appropriate etiquette and behaviors.

Big Steps

- Use billboards, radio spots, and local television ads to publicize changes in expectations regarding infant and toddler behavior.
- Use social media to celebrate the changes in the culture of the library regarding services to families.
- When redesigning children's spaces, include commercially available noise-absorbing materials. Any soft surface helps to absorb sound.

EMOTIONS AND CARE PROVIDERS

To provide excellent service to families with small children, it is imperative to understand the emotional dynamics taking place in their everyday world. Family life is a complex mix of competing emotional states. The joy, sadness, wistfulness, mild resentment, jealousy, and pride that come with bringing a baby into the world are competing for expression. For first-time parents, delivering their child changes their very self-definition from couple to family. This shift alone can be a challenge as they can no longer "up and go" the way they did before. Now, the baby and all her demands must be taken into consideration.

A closer look at the family may show that mom is exhausted from lack of sleep, which makes her more emotionally vulnerable. And although she is thrilled to introduce her four-month-old to the world, she is already a bit sad that she no longer has a newborn. Her two-year-old is at once possessive of and annoyed by his new sibling, who is taking up too much of mommy's time. Daddy may feel overwhelmingly proud yet a little left out as mommy nurses. And now they are at the library, looking for a change of scenery and a bit of a break from being cooped up in the house. A lot has happened in their world over the last few months.

At about the four-month mark, families, especially first-time parents, are becoming more confident with handling their baby. Also, at this milestone, parents and baby are completely smitten with each other. Their "in-love-ness" can sometimes be as annoying as that teenage couple in the young adult section of the library! Nevertheless, it is what should be expected at this point in their lives. Sensitive librarians acknowledge this phenomenon and gracefully tolerate it, echoing the "oohs" and "ahhs" that the family is exuding. And proud adults need to share their pictures and stories. The feelings that parents are experiencing for their little ones run deep. The love bonds they are all establishing will continue to grow right along with the ongoing maturity of their child.

Mothers

Library service specific to new mothers and mothers of small children isn't often discussed, but it should be considered more fully, especially in respect to their emotional world. A lot is going on in the mother's heart, as who she is and how she defines herself has changed considerably since the birth of her first child. Becoming a mother is (usually) a profound experience in a woman's life.

The physical experience of pregnancy brings with it alterations in her body. The growing as-yet-unborn child and the changes the woman's body makes as it adapts to her baby's needs are all part of a unique time in her life. Childbirth itself, at the very least, is traumatic to the mother's body and involves a unique set of physical and hormonal occurrences. The post-delivery recovery process includes mending, restoration, and readjustment to the pre-pregnancy state. Hormone swings, combined with the stress of adjustment to a new normal, come with the package. Difficulties, such as an unexpected cesarean delivery or the birth of a child with developmental issues, complicate matters.

The new mother may have been well prepared from an intellectual standpoint for the physical changes her body is going through. However, it is difficult, if not impossible, to prepare herself for the emotional impact. For most mothers, meeting sweet, long-anticipated baby for the first time is a heartbreaking experience in the best sense of the word. In an instant, she is no longer the center of her own universe. It has now been taken over by the awe-invoking yet needful little one, and the new mother's ability to self-sacrifice has just taken a colossal leap. New mothers may still be experiencing waves of post-labor exhaustion. Also, as is commonly the case, they are tired from disrupted sleep schedules. Some new moms have difficulty in adapting emotionally to the enormity of this new role. Some may experience postpartum depression. (Not at all an uncommon event, it nevertheless can go undetected, placing undue stress on the new family as mom struggles to cope.) Daily routines are altered as baby and mother become more acquainted. Eventually, perhaps needing to get out of the house and seeking a safe, comfortable place, she and her baby bravely decide to visit the library.

Veteran moms also have unique concerns. They now have a new member of the family to work into the routine while they are mothering an older child or two. Every child is different, and getting adjusted to various personalities can be a challenge. This may be especially true if mom had an easy time of it with the first baby. A colicky, temperamental, or generally fussy newborn may throw mom off her emotional balance as she tries to get the family to bond. When she brings her family to the library, she has the opportunity to hear others' stories from their home fronts along with coping strategies. It is often the case that mothers with babies and toddlers are genuinely glad to be in one another's company and, for a little while, are relieved of some stress. Often they return home from the library with newly acquired suggestions or ideas to put into practice.

Fathers

Most children's librarians are thrilled to see dads in the library because they tend to visit less often than mothers. Especially noteworthy are dads braving the library alone with babies and toddlers. In today's society, libraries are seeing more stay-at-home dads who are looking for healthy, inexpensive, daytime destinations. Some fathers are full-time, custodial, single parents looking for safe and welcoming places. Reaching dads as potential patrons is a bit challenging because fathers aren't as likely to view the children's library as a male-friendly environment. Old stereotypes regarding librarians are alive and well, and fathers, especially those who may have had negative public school experiences that reinforced those stereotypes, are especially impacted.

Many fathers do not view themselves as readers, even though they may read quite a bit. Perhaps they do not typically enjoy reading, say, a novel, but will read the newspaper, a repair manual, or a website with great attention. Because he doesn't necessarily think he's a reader, dad may feel very much out of his element. Although dad may be concerned with his child's general education, he might view the library as a positive thing only despite, not because of, his own experience. However, serving fathers can be a great joy. Often, dads who bravely enter the children's library are going against their comfort zone but are truly concerned with the well-being of their children. Dads, too, can be mildly self-deprecating and awkward but conduct themselves with a gentle sense of humor and with respect for the library as an institution.

For this book, I approached many fathers, both library users and nonusers, and asked about their feelings regarding visits with their infants and toddlers. Most of them who use the library reported that they enjoy their visits if they feel a strong sense of welcome and if their children are not perceived as a nuisance. Many stated that they wouldn't seek out a librarian but appreciated being approached, welcomed, properly introduced, and invited to join in any activities. More independent, or even a bit shy, they tend to want to hang back, observe, and just enjoy the children's room with their charges, and not engage too heavily with others, at least not at first. Also, dads tend to be more conservative in how many items they choose to borrow, or whether they borrow at all, voicing concern that they won't be able to keep track of things as well as, say, mom would and are not willing to face whatever embarrassment that might cause.

It is an asset, for sure, to see healthy father-child relationships in the library. It is also worth mentioning that even somewhat negligent fathers can be positively impacted by casual visits to the library. Some are just looking for an Internet connection so they can play video games on their phone, kid in tow. Once in the area, however, dad becomes introduced to the rich resources of the children's library of which he was formerly unaware. He may also find an ally and friend in the librarian.

Many of the fathers interviewed said that it never occurred to them to take the kids to the library, especially really young ones. Often, the look on their faces indicated near panic! Some also presented the sadly surprising, albeit understandable, concern that they are very cautious to be around *any* little children's area without adult female accompaniment due to any negative interpretations that might result. Children's librarians can go the extra heroic mile for first-time visiting dads by making the initial move toward introductions and offering a quick review of the library's holdings and general floor plan. Helping dad feel at home in the library with his children, acknowledging that "kids will be kids," sends the message that he, too, has found a place of respite, acceptance, and support. And he'll probably be back—soon.

Other Care Providers

Care providers come in a wide variety of ages and capabilities, and with their own emotional issues. Further, the quality of their care can vary widely, as most children's librarians can attest. Some caregivers are twelve-year-old siblings or babysitters, still quite immature themselves. Some are grandparents, and even great-grandparents, with child-care responsibilities thrust upon them even as their own adult child may be dealing with drug addiction, terminal illness, or prison time. Some are private babysitting service providers with a few too many to manage. Care providers may also be foster families, visiting noncustodial parents, or doting aunties and uncles. All of them clamor into the library with their own emotional situations of the day and of the moment.

Babies and toddlers are attuned and highly sensitive to the emotional cues and clues of whomever is providing their care. Using their sharp observational skills, the little ones react and respond to the varying emotional states of their caregivers. If the adult is agitated, the baby may be fussy and clingy. If exuberant, the child may be rambunctious, and if calm, the child may be more sedate. Librarians interacting with this wildly diverse population are in a unique situation in that they are also entering into, reading, responding to, and interacting with this already complex dynamic (see the feature "Positive Interventions"). Why would librarians even want to enter into this unpredictable mix of human emotions? Of course, the answer is because children's librarians truly care about the emotional health and well-being of all their patrons.

EASING EMOTIONS OF CARE PROVIDERS

Librarians daily provide the easily overlooked service of positively impacting the emotional lives of patrons. This is perhaps even more true for families with young children. It takes a lot of courage to bring a new baby out into the public arena, especially for first-time parents. The children's librarian has the potential to instill confidence and to encourage healthy emotional development for these families. She may also be a great source of referral to community support because she may be first to pick up on parents' needs and suspect a problem.

Positive Interventions

Sadie, mother of seven-month-old Bridget, identified the library as a safe public place for a court-ordered, supervised parental visitation. As a result, Bridget visited the library only occasionally and at set times with mother and visiting father. The entire event was stressful for Bridget, and she cried most of the time. After a few such visits, the librarians became aware of the negative message this was sending to Bridget and were genuinely concerned for everyone's mental health. In an attempt to create a more positive library experience for Bridget, the librarians decided to intervene. Sadie was encouraged to bring the baby to the library under happier circumstances because Bridget was learning to associate the library with emotionally negative events. As trust was established, Sadie began to share a bit of her story, exhibiting a certain amount of fear in relation to her personal life. The librarian was able to provide Sadie with local health and safety protection and support information, which was gratefully received. Now Bridget and her mother frequently visit the library under happier circumstances. They are both learning that the library is a good and positive place to be.

Baby Steps

- Create simple brochures with contact information for local service agencies and make them available within the children's play area so they can be accessed anonymously.
- Encourage staff members from other departments to refer new parents to the children's area.
- Greet new mothers and fathers with honest enthusiasm.
- Inquire about the new mother's overall health and adjustment, exhibiting a level of sympathy and compassion. Ask how dad is doing, too.
- Offer tactfully empathetic words to parents, if it is in keeping with the situation, to help ease any embarrassment on their part. Comments such as "I see Johnny is thoroughly stating his opinion today" send a message of understanding and acceptance to the parent.
- Hone your sense of humor in emotionally charged situations, if appropriate. A light interpretation can ease a tense situation.
- Create programs that are loosely structured and open-ended, such as new mothers' meet-and-greet sessions, play dates, and casual support groups.
- Invite community partners to be on hand to introduce themselves and to offer assistance.

- Host a reception for new families during which librarians can introduce themselves and share what the library has to offer.

Big Steps

- Become involved in community family support networks, thereby making associations and referrals more personal, applicable, and accurate.
- Create workshops, attend meetings, or otherwise encourage continuing education in the area of emotional health through your professional library organization.
- Attend conferences, workshops, webinars, or meetings outside the normal library offerings that address emotional health.
- Attend lectures or courses on the subject of differing cultural family dynamics and how they express themselves.
- Implement any interior design changes within budgetary limitations, such as new window treatments, a fresh coat of paint, or a better-lit foyer, to evoke a welcoming feel.

SIBLING EMOTIONS MATTER, TOO

Toddler siblings present yet another dynamic in the emotional life of the family. Depending on countless other factors, the adjustment of a sibling to his new baby is also emotionally charged. He may feel protective of "his" baby, threatened, or even indifferent. He may also be overlooked and even ignored as everyone makes a fuss over the baby and forgets he's even in the room. Good service to these new big brothers or sisters most certainly should involve acknowledging them when being introduced to the new arrival.

Under such circumstances, toddlers and preschoolers might act out inappropriately, not really because they are "being bad" but because they, too, are adjusting to a new definition of normal. They want to be noticed and acknowledged. For example, the four-year-old may "borrow" (yank) a toy from another child. The two-year-old might steal the baby's pacifier, be clingy, or become quite shy and hide behind her adult. Mom and dad are aware of these somewhat embarrassing moments but are also struggling to keep it all together. Patience with these behaviors is not only necessary but also greatly valued.

For the librarian, being attentive to the delicate emotional climate of the growing family is a primary professional skill to hone (see the feature "The Power of Distraction"). It is an important part of establishing the trust necessary to provide ongoing service. Although emotional awareness is certainly the norm

The Power of Distraction

Twenty-two-month-old Nicole was playing in the library along with her four-year-old brother, Colton. In a few short weeks, there would be a new sibling in the family. In preparing to leave the library after a session of play, Nicole began to cry, feeling a mix of frustration, hunger, tiredness, and unwillingness. The tears turned torrential, intense, inconsolable—and loud! The librarian asked Colton if he wanted to offer a tissue to mom to help mop up Nicole's tears. Then the librarian asked him if he wanted a sticker. Nicole was instantly distracted and interested by what Colton and the librarian were doing. She stopped crying and received a sticker from mom's hand, and the family finished preparing for their exit without further incident. The effort at indirect, positive distraction worked! This time, anyway. And an appreciative mom offered a smile and a whispered "Thank you" to the librarian.

across the librarianship landscape, the lifelong impact it can have on families with small children cannot be overstated.

Quality service to babies and toddlers includes caring about the feelings of siblings. As they witness adult interactions with their siblings, they learn how to better understand their own emotional lives and to respect the feelings of others.

Baby Steps

- Invite big brother to introduce you to his new sister, as it acknowledges his presence and relationship to the baby.
- Display an interest in him individually, not just in the context of a new sibling.
- Keep a small inventory of special stickers for big brothers and big sisters.

Big Steps

- Have a Birth-day Party and celebrate siblings, too. Make it an annual event!
- Take a class or a refresher course on all that is involved in delivering and caring for babies and toddlers.

- Attend a workshop or conference dealing with special issues, needs, and dynamics among siblings, such as how to deal with autism or Down syndrome.

FEELING FOR FAMILIES

Sometimes, even unintentionally, libraries project messages of emotional neutrality or, perhaps, even negativity, disdain, or annoyance where babies and their caregivers are concerned. However, creating and sustaining positive emotional library environments is an important part of quality service to this (and every other) population. Fostering these positive messages extends well beyond the role of the children's librarian, incorporating the contributions and interactions of the entire library staff and administration. Babies and toddlers are quick to discern the emotional ambience of their surroundings and will resonate with that mood in their own developing ways.

Libraries are devoted to serving the informational needs of their patrons. Although this goal is usually the overt understanding of library service, there is most likely much more going on covertly in the lives of patrons. People come to the library for information on how to plan a wedding, cope with cancer, manage a death, recover from abuse, celebrate a holiday, and so many other emotionally laden situations. Librarians know this well and, as professionals, provide information tactfully, compassionately, and discreetly, mindful of the patron's emotional state. This outstanding service model should also be extended to the emotionally pulsing world of families with babies and toddlers.

Note

1. Jay Geidd, "The Teen Brain: Insights from Neuroimaging," *Journal of Adolescent Health* 42, no. 4 (April 2008): 335–43.

INTELLECTUAL PURSUITS
Learning for Babies and Families

THE HUMAN BABY COMES INTO THE WORLD WITH AN AMAZING, unfinished brain that is prepared to learn about the world, and with a passionate desire to do so. At birth, the baby brain contains about a hundred billion neurons, about the same as an adult. However, unlike the adult brain, the neurons are not yet connected to each other. Known as synaptogenesis, the axon-dendrite connections of the neurons occur over time and with repeated experiences. By the time the infant is two years old, a single neuron may have generated as many as ten thousand different connections to other cells. It is easy to overlook this remarkable accomplishment, as babies seem to learn so effortlessly and quickly. The most basic of these neuron connections, such as recognizing and responding to mother's voice, experiencing the physical sensations of hot and cold, learning the difference between being upright and prone, and countless others, are being made every waking moment.[1]

Although this flurry of growth begins long before birth, baby's developing brain is poised to learn through the broader contexts baby will encounter. The growing child's intellectual development will be influenced by mild sensory stimulations, immediate environments, and social interactions. Neuronal growth is further impacted by the baby's unique genetic heritage and temperament. In some respects, these environmental, sensory, and social experiences are required for optimal development. All the players in the complex process work together to influence and build the infrastructure of a baby's brain.

INTELLECTUAL GROWTH: THE DEVELOPMENTAL TIME LINE

Even at birth, the newborn knows a few things. For example, baby can distinguish the rhythm and cadence of her native language from those of other languages, having heard her mother's speech patterns while still in the womb. Baby can also identify her mother's scent over that of other women. In only four weeks, the developing baby is able to make out the elements of the human face and prefers viewing faces over other objects. By six weeks, she begins to display her ability to imitate things she observes.

By ten weeks, baby is able to distinguish individual objects and understand that some things move while other things are stationary. She will track with her eyes even if an object "disappears" behind another object and then reappears, indicating the ability to anticipate and predict. As early as fourteen weeks, baby knows that tall objects cannot hide behind short objects. She can also keep the representation of an object in her mind even if she can no longer see it, displaying her awareness of some basic rules of logic. Baby is also demonstrating preference, as she makes raking gestures, grasps, and then draws objects to her mouth for further study.

By four months, baby practices intense observational skills. She knows her name and will turn toward someone calling for her. She studies with fascination her fingers, touching, manipulating, wiggling, and turning them. Soon she will display problem-solving behaviors and will be persistent in her desire to understand, for instance, how to retrieve a toy hidden under a blanket. She is also playfully making noises, trying out speech sounds, and discovering that "da-da" or "mum-mum" vocalizations create results that can be manipulated to her advantage. Clever indeed, in just a few months of learning!

By eight to twelve months, the pre- or early walker is busily observing, interacting, practicing, and playing with keen intent. She uses the pincer grasp to retrieve tiny objects that she studies with eyes, fingers, and mouth. She uses her ever-more-mobile body to further explore, discover, reach, and examine. At this time, she will follow an adult's pointing finger and gaze in order to home in on what the adult is bringing to her attention. She displays preferences and begins to use pointing behaviors herself. When manipulating books, for example, she will return to a favorite title, lift flaps, touch textures, and point to objects that appeal to her. She will also be attentive to an adult's pointing to a page, indicating the ability to exchange interests.

At the twelve- to eighteen-month stage, independence and autonomy begin to assert themselves, and the once-compliant baby becomes more outspoken in response to her environment. She is now walking, even running, and is fascinated by anything that catches her eye. She understands and begins to use the word "no." The now-toddler or early walker will respond quickly by waving bye-bye or blowing a kiss. She is also beginning to use the vocabulary words to which she has been exposed, saying things like "ball" to indicate her desire to play with her ball. She is making connections between speech and action, and she will, for example, throw a ball when encouraged to do so. She is quite busy acquiring, practicing, and beginning to use the spoken word. Baby is conducting science experiments through her play, discovering the laws of gravity, cause and effect, balance, and action-reaction. She is actively naming things and vocalizes her preference to "do it by myself."

By eighteen months to two years of age, the toddler has already accomplished many things, such as physical locomotion, use of the spoken word along with a variety of other communication methods, and application of some of the basic workings of the physical laws of the universe. She is also becoming self-aware, thus ushering in the next level of development—self-consciousness. From reflexive action to self-consciousness, the remarkable intellectual growth during the first few months of life is accomplished, and at an astounding rate. Parents and caregivers are so very proud of all these milestones, and the professional librarian's expectation and reward is to be an active influence and participant in these processes.

LIBRARY "SCHOOL" FOR BABY

As most people would agree, the public library celebrates, encourages, and supports lifelong learning. For the most part, *learning* tends to be viewed as a rather formal, academic, or hands-on endeavor, somewhat limited to the subject being taught or explored, such as reading, swimming, or gardening. In this more pedestrian way of defining learning, it is seen as a positive thing. However, in the broader, psychological sense of the word, *learning* is defined as the process of neurons making synaptic connections to other neurons. It is a whole-brain, physiological, nondiscriminating, and morally neutral event. It is further influenced by one's individual perceptions, temperament, heredity, environment, and culture. Repeated experiences make these neuronal connections transfer faster and stronger. Effective learning, therefore, requires repeated positive experiences. This is the stuff of good habits, happy patterns of daily life, and rich, thriving encounters across the developmental landscape. Sadly, the opposite also holds true: poor environments, little social interaction, and lack of stimulation diminish the budding quality of the developing brain.

Thus, being in a library has the potential to positively influence baby's brain growth, as the very ambience of a public library celebrates all things associated with books. The children's library, in particular, creates an atmosphere that is especially interesting to young patrons, including babies and toddlers, thus making their area of the library an even greater potential learning experience. If the definition of learning, as indicated earlier, is widened to include the whole-brain experience that babies are realizing, the children's library emerges as a place in which baby can be schooled. Babies' learning processes are thereby influenced by every encounter within the library walls.

Babies who are fortunate enough to visit this, the library-as-school, regularly during the first years of life are making those repeated neuronal connections.

A Librarian Observes Learning

Afterlearning about several of the capabilities of babies, one librarian reported that she found those claims rather difficult to believe. So, to test the facts, she began to experiment. For example, she approached adults who had babies in carriers and asked the name and age of each baby. She then watched the infants from the side as she called to them. Repeatedly, infants about three and a half to four months old turned their heads, seeking out her face and making eye contact. These babies, indeed, knew their own names, acknowledged that someone was calling to them, and turned toward that voice.

The librarian also engaged in brief, simple board book play with babies who were about eight months old. For example, she pointed at objects, without comment, and observed as babies followed her finger and focused their gaze, then reached for the object to which she was pointing. She approached babies with a picture book open to an illustration of a mother and baby elephant and ask her little patrons to show her where the baby was. Much to her surprise, most babies would open a hand and cover the picture of the baby elephant. When sharing pictures in books, babies repeatedly followed her lead, touching pictures of interest and even trying to "lift" objects from the page as they struggled to learn the difference between the real object and the symbol that the book represented. Babies would also point, lift flaps, and otherwise engage physically with the books while occasionally scanning her face for reaction. Again and again, babies would return to books of their preference, pushing aside other books offered to them.

Becoming more aware of the enormous learning that was transpiring and observing it in action made a believer of the librarian. Summing up her experiences, the librarian claimed that she was both humbled and awed by babies' heretofore unrecognized (by her) abilities. She also reported being somewhat embarrassed by not realizing all that was transpiring in their little minds. Librarianship has taken a decided turn for her, as she continues to include these basic interactive encounters with babies, knowing that the impact is much greater than she ever would have guessed.

For these developing young patrons, positive experiences in libraries hold tremendous potential for assisting them in their intellectual pursuits right from the very beginning. Furthermore, children's librarians can then be defined not so much as teachers but as facilitators of learning. Within the professional role of children's librarianship, they possess the ability to make a positive impact, not just while delivering programs but by virtue of *every* encounter (see the feature "A Librarian Observes Learning").

Providing for healthy intellectual growth in the library is almost effortless. It simply amounts to being cognizant and respectful of the process and acknowledging it as it presents itself. With awareness and a few simple tools, librarians can provide entry-level, quality "educational" experiences for babies and toddlers any and every time they are in the library.

Baby Steps

- Encourage repeat visits in order to foster the neuronal connections to long-term relationships, perhaps lifelong.
- Provide *access* to books so that babies are able to reach for them independently.
- Raise the level of awareness of and respect for the intellectual capabilities of babies.
- Actively engage with families in the play process, even if only for a few minutes. This participation shows that you take them all seriously and that their being in the library is more important to you than whatever it is they think you might be doing "at the desk."
- Capture baby's learning process in the library on video and, with permission of the adult, share it on social media or the library's website, linking theory to actual learning events.
- Comment to adults about what you are observing in keeping with baby's brain development.

Big Steps

- Request or host workshops and seminars devoted to the topic of infant and early childhood intellectual development.
- Take a class, a refresher class, or a workshop at your local college or university. New research is being published regularly on this topic.
- Create promotional, educational media devoted to the topic of educating babies in libraries and disseminate the products through ob-gyns' and pediatricians' offices.

- Devote a portion of your library website to this topic, providing links to more information on the subject.

BABY AS INFORMATION GATHERER

Librarianship is all about gathering information. Teaching about, and assisting others in, the process of acquiring information is an important part of the profession, and one that most librarians hold in high regard. However, the process is a bit different when assisting an infant to be an information gatherer. Christina Doyle has identified several components involved in the process of gathering information. Applying these various components to the intellectually developing infant gives them broader meaning.

According to Doyle, the information gatherer does the following:

- Recognizes that accurate and complete information is the basis for intelligent decision making
- Recognizes the need for information
- Evaluates information
- Organizes information for practical application
- Integrates new information into an existing body of knowledge
- Uses information in critical thinking and problem solving[2]

Babies are gathering information from everywhere, all the time! For example, when the seven-week-old infant is fiercely concentrating on the librarian's face as the librarian engages in conversation with her, she is "integrating new information into an existing body of knowledge." The six-month-old manipulating a board book, finding out that it only opens one way, is indeed evaluating information and organizing it for practical application. According to Alan Fogel, "infants use touching, listening, watching, and mouthing as alternative sources of information gathering."[3] Thus, any and all activity that occurs within the library setting is rife with information-gathering potential.

Children's librarians have a unique opportunity here. As they broaden their understanding of typical information gathering to include physical interaction and every single aspect of the baby's visit, they are excellently situated to channel all this active potential in positive and purposeful directions (see the feature "Delight in Word Play"). By providing meaningful encounters and mildly stimulating play areas, they encourage and advance babies' efforts in this regard. Thus, the children's library as a *place* perhaps should be viewed as an information-gathering *experience*. In ways heretofore unrecognized, or at the very least underutilized, perceiving the baby as an information gatherer also alters

Delight in Word Play

Kate is a librarian aware of the value of introducing words to babies. On one particular visit, her little eleven-month-old friend Brianna "gifted" her with a library puppet from the puppet bin. As she received the puppet, Kate exclaimed, "Exquisite!" For reasons known only to Brianna, this exchange sent her into a fit of giggles. The game was on! Back for more puppets! With each puppet delivered, a new exclamation was offered—"Intriguing!" "Imaginative!" "Stupendous!" "Regal!"—with Brianna emitting delightful squeals at each turn. The play continued for a full ten minutes, as Kate, immensely amused, groped for more and more words to share. In the meantime, Brianna's mommy and auntie were observing the event, fully entertained by the episode. Further, as Kate awaited the arrival of the next puppet gift, she and the adults discussed the learning that was transpiring. This happy, chance encounter of a baby offering a gift to the librarian had the unintended consequence of introducing little Brianna to a host of rarely encountered vocabulary words. The event was also a very positive experience, creating deep connections in Brianna's brain to words, librarians, families, and libraries in the best sense. Finally, it gave mommy and auntie inspiration for how this enriching exercise could be enjoyed at home. Did they have fun? Absolutely! Was it meaningful? Most assuredly.

the standard for professional service. Every encounter with the very *person* who is a children's librarian fulfills this information-gathering need.

Being an information provider to babies takes children's librarianship down a fresh and compelling path. Generally speaking, librarianship engages in rather intuitive practices, as most librarians would attest—more so, perhaps, for children's librarians. Serving infants and toddlers builds on those intuitive abilities and may require the honing of one's talents.

Baby Steps

- See yourself as an information provider to babies, honoring their requests and information-gathering needs as much as those of any other patron by learning the ways in which babies communicate their needs, such as by pointing, staring, grunting, or just extending a little hand in your direction.
- Study babies in action, especially watching infants' eyes and expressions, as that is how they best communicate, keeping in mind that every child is unique.

- Hone your observational skills. Much can be learned about what babies are accomplishing just by learning to recognize what you see.
- Spend some time with another children's librarian carefully observing babies at play in the library. Take notes on what you see. Share your notes with each other, expanding on the experience.
- Invite others outside the field of librarianship to do the same observation exercise and then share your observations.
- Invite administrators to do the observation exercise, illuminating the learning that is transpiring as it unfolds in front of them.

Big Steps

- Invite professionals to facilitate workshops for parents on the intrinsic value of play, making the infant and toddler part of the program.
- Take a field trip to a local children's museum, preschool, playground, or other facility where babies and caregivers are actively engaged with their surroundings. While there, study the activity of babies engaged in play in these other situations, seeing what works and why. This observation may inspire minor yet valuable changes in your existing children's area.
- Build a library-appropriate play area that allows for intellectual pursuits and that is always available, regardless of staff hours or special equipment.

BABY AS SCIENTIST: LEARNING SCIENCE, TECHNOLOGY, ENGINEERING, ART, AND MATH (STEAM)

The term *cognition* is often used interchangeably with the phrase *intellectual development*. More specifically, though, *cognition* "refers to all the mental processes, such as thinking, remembering, use of language, problem solving, and concept formation. The cognitive processes thus make up the functional component of intelligence."[4] Infant learning in this regard is accomplished through cognitive information-acquiring avenues of baby-initiated experiments, intense and rich interactions, observations, and experiences. These experiences are defined by adults as *play.*

Of course, all creatures learn, but human babies also have the capacity to *think* about the things they are learning, and researchers are beginning to discover that this capacity to think begins much earlier than was previously believed. For example, even as early as the age of four months, babies will become bored very quickly when shown a video clip of a routine event. However, they will stop, stare, and even whimper with confusion when shown the same video clip altered to include an impossible event, such as an object being suspended in space. This behavior indicates that, even at such an early age, infants know the difference between what is possible and what is impossible. Young discerners indeed![5]

Babies are also incredibly creative. They try any number of self-generated actions in order to investigate, communicate, participate, experiment, and engage in their world. A cracker might be used as a hammer, a ball as a puzzle piece, or a set of keys as a rattle. Adults tend to overlook these activities as simply "babies at play," but it is doubtful baby has ever witnessed anyone using a cracker as a hammer. Baby has just demonstrated his ability to be innovative, to use tools, and to independently problem solve. Child development experts often discourage use of battery-operated toys because they rob little children of creative activity. With all the bells and whistles provided for them, children don't have the opportunity to invent their own. After all, if the car makes an electronic "vroom-vroom" sound, baby won't need to imagine and voice a sound of her own.

Babies and toddlers are integrating immense amounts of information. They are learning the natural laws of the universe, such as gravity, cause and effect, mass, weight, balance, and torque. They are also learning the contrasts of light and dark, day and night, hot and cold, big and little, up and down, stop and go, and so on. There is knowledge of shape, color, size, and texture to be gained. Babies are examining the differences in the properties of elements such as wood, metal, plastic, stone, and ceramic. They are grasping quantity, quality, and sequencing. They are also trying to understand what is possible and impossible, to separate fact from fiction, and to incorporate the language needed to describe these phenomena.

These play trials can easily be described as science experiments, and the lessons they teach are the natural result. Babies, through their dogged, repeated, and artistically clever play experiences, are learning fundamental science, technology, engineering, and mathematics principles that operate in their everyday world. All these lessons are learned naturally and exquisitely through interactions with the world around them.

In addition, baby's physical body needs to be discovered, understood, controlled, commanded, and explored. Through practice, practice, and more practice, as the neurons and synapses lay deep traces in the brain, baby is learning to coordinate her *physical* body with her *mental* goals, and at astonishing speeds. For instance, she will engage her mind and body with the full concentration necessary to retrieve a toy by focusing on it, aiming at it, reaching for it, grasping it, and finally pulling it to her mouth for further inspection. She makes it look so easy, but even this simple sequence of events takes a long time and repeated practice to master.

Such is the difficult, intriguing, and learning stuff of play. Baby is musing such things as, "What are those interesting wiggly things at the end of my arm?"

and "Water is hard to catch!" She is trying to keep her balance, hold the handle of a little shopping cart, *and* take a halting step, all at the same time. There are so many questions that need to be answered and so many experiments to perform. When the library provides interactive experiences through play, it is furthering this general knowledge base.

In addition, by making available toys, games, puppets, and other tools of exploration, libraries expand on what baby is learning at home. Many babies come from impoverished learning environments, making the library one of the few places they can truly experience such complex elements.

Basic infant and toddler toys have been popular for ages because they are intrinsically interesting. Block play, for example, is never boring to children, as they create, imagine, stack, and tumble a tower. Yet this form of play provides dozens of learning and creating opportunities. Children are learning about fractions, cause and effect, ramps, inclines, gravity, and balance. Rainmaker tube toys are also intrinsically interesting, engaging baby in tactile, visual, and auditory stimulation as he learns how to use the forces of gravity to manipulate the object. The opportunity to paint with water, pudding, or applesauce introduces baby to the qualities of viscosity. On and on it goes. The value of play in learning scientific principles cannot be overemphasized, yet it is so very easy for adults to overlook and underestimate. Perhaps this is so because the little ones are having so much fun. And the astute librarian can usually suggest a book or two so the play and learning are further advanced.

Learning about the value of play as a means of understanding the world is fascinating and entertaining. Children's librarians are highly encouraged to pursue more information regarding the merits of play.

Baby Steps

- Put words to your observations and describe what is being learned.
- Watch for examples of babies' experimentation while at play, observing the thinking and concentration evident in their faces, becoming more sensitive to their learning processes.
- Equip your spaces with safe manipulatives, such as building blocks, dolls, puzzles, puppets, or simple wooden toys, being careful to avoid anything that may present a choking or pinching hazard. Only a few at a time are necessary.
- Avoid purchasing battery-operated toys.
- Keep a small collection of such toys in storage and swap them out from time to time to heighten interest.
- Become better informed about what is being learned through various play media and toys.

- Enter into the play randomly, even if only for a few minutes. Your actions will prove to caregivers your deep commitment to and respect for this population.
- Model simple and appropriate play to caregivers, some of whom truly don't know how to play with their babies.
- Tell baby what she is learning: "You found out that the little ball fits, but the big one doesn't!"
- Extend the learning, making suggestions such as, "I wonder what will happen if you put the block on the top?"
- Educate administration and support staff about the deep value of play so that your involvement in these activities is taken seriously and seen as necessary to quality service.

Big Steps

- Install an electronic device that scrolls messages and images indicating what baby is learning through various forms of play.
- Attend a workshop or class on the value of play.
- Collaborate with local children's museums, perhaps borrowing from them portable, interactive, science-based learning stations for very young children.
- Support and promote events at other libraries and museums, and perhaps create a loan system between institutions.
- Visit a children's museum for inspiration and, if possible, interview exhibit designers regarding the research they employed.

BABY AS PRE-LITERACY LANGUAGE LEARNER

Of particular interest to librarians, infant learning includes the acquisition of oral language, the precursor to the spoken and written word. Saroj Ghoting and Pamela Martin-Diaz state that "[o]ral language, which encompasses listening, speaking, and verbal communication, is the foundation for both early literacy and later literacy. It is not considered a component because, quite simply, it suffuses all the early literacy components."[6] Before there can be reading, there must be language acquisition, including the development of oral language. In other words, the baby must learn to *use* this language himself. As baby proceeds through the various stages of language acquisition, the infant-turned-toddler is also taking active steps toward learning to read.

Learning the language of one's native culture is one of the most valuable of all learning processes because it allows for the human capacity to communicate.

Language is defined as a complex system of mutually agreed-upon symbols used to express and understand ideas and feelings. In its broadest meaning, language refers to an act or acts that produce some kind of interchange or communication between two or more people. The symbols used in language include vocal utterances, written expressions, and bodily movements such as hand gestures and facial expressions. *Speech,* on the other hand, is the vocal or oral component of language and refers to the production of spoken words or other meaningful sounds.[7]

How does this process transpire? Research indicates that, while still in the uterus, babies hear the muffled sounds of their native language, primarily through the amplification of the mother's voice through the amniotic fluid. A newborn can distinguish the cadence and rhythm of his native language over those of other languages. He also responds more strongly to some speech sounds and rhythms over others, indicating an innate ability to distinguish grammatical rules. From birth, all babies can learn any given language, and, as their hearing develops, they begin to identify the full spectrum of speech sounds (see the feature "Undetected Hearing Loss"). As early as six months of age, though, this ability is greatly reduced as the brain focuses on the primary language of the infant's culture.

Researchers have discovered, however, that the language acquisition process requires *active* listening to, repeating after, interpreting, and eventually speaking with *others.* Infants and toddlers simply engrossed in visual media are not learning language, even though it would seem that they should be. Engagement with, and the vocalization of, one's primary language needs to be physically, actively exercised. It is not a passive process. It involves the development of fine muscle control and movements in and of the mouth and various other places in the body from which words are formed, heard, pronounced, and practiced. Language also involves studying others' faces while learning nuances and inflections of tone, cadence, rhythm, and emphases in speech. There are commands, questions, statements, exclamations, and verbalized emotional expressions to decipher. The growing vocabulary consists of such components as prepositions, names, objects, actions, and descriptors. With all there is to know and learn, it is nothing short of astonishing that, as early as three months of age, baby recognizes and responds to her own name.[8]

Written language, although similar to spoken language, "sounds" slightly different. Hearing the written word offers babies an opportunity to learn this "dialect" through the tones, patterns, and rhythms that are different from those of the spoken word. For example, in speech, phrases such as "he said" or "she exclaimed" are not used. These phrases, along with dozens of others, are used only in writing and, therefore, are met only when reading. Any exposure a baby has to the different nuances of written language will be foundationally laid in

Undetected Hearing Loss

One serious challenge to language learning arises when babies incur mild hearing loss. This loss can be the result of ear infections, noise pollution, loud amplification in vehicles, use of headphones, allergies, and many other situations. The phenomenon is frequently overlooked because it is difficult to detect. The lack of ability to hear nuances of language can have enormous impact when the child encounters formal learning situations. For instance, mild hearing loss may not allow the toddler to hear the subtle difference between the "sl" and "fl" phonemes, making it difficult to identify and decode them later when the child is actively learning to read. The library can be an agent of change for these at-risk children simply by bringing the situation to the attention of parents and encouraging them to have their children assessed. Providing simple signage, creating an informational brochure, or adding a note in the monthly newsletter about the importance of screenings are all ways in which to make the unsuspecting care provider aware of this issue and its connection to reading.*

* Listening and Spoken Language Knowledge Center, "The Speech Banana," www.agbell.org/Speech-Banana; "From Language to Literacy," www.agbell.org/Document.aspx?id=464; "Communication: How Babies Learn," www.agbell.org/Document.aspx?id=225.

the brain, making it easier to assimilate the "language" of reading at a later date. For the uninitiated, it seems quite silly to read the poetic writing of Shakespeare, the idiomatic works of Mark Twain, the lilting and lofty cadences of poetry, the straightforward words of the local newspaper, the technical language of a repair manual, or any other genre of writing to babies. However, as just described, hearing the language of the written word from very early on creates the brain-based groundwork for optimal success at a much later date.

Baby is also beginning to grasp the meaning of symbols. Understanding the nature of symbols is a result of play and is indicative of a very abstract skill. It is a precursor to reading because words, both written and spoken, are symbols that express meaningful communication. The word *cat*, for instance, represents a physical cat. When baby recognizes a picture, whether realistic or cartoonish, as that of a cat, she is grasping the idea of symbolic representation, yet another step toward literacy. Further, if the adult points to a picture of a cat and says "cat" and the eighteen-month-old makes a "meow" sound, the toddler has made a huge mental leap into the world of symbols.

These accomplishments are all achieved in the first (and in only) two years. Emphasizing the acquisition of the various letters of the standard alphabet, Ghoting and Martin-Diaz elevate this rapid development to an even higher pitch. They report that "[t]o distinguish one letter from another, children need to pay attention to what makes letters different rather than what makes them similar. This *insight begins at about two and a half years old and develops as children encounter print in their environment*" (emphasis added).[9] From barely hearing and forming the concepts of language to early letter recognition in only thirty or so months is indeed profound pre- and early literacy acquisition.

Children's librarians have long championed the focused goal of raising readers. Virginia Walter states that "[w]hen other professionals look at the inhabitants of their domains schoolteachers see students; social workers see dependent members of a family structure; soccer coaches see young athletes; pediatricians see healthy children and sick children; police officers see good children and bad ones; marketing experts see customers. Children's librarians see readers."[10] Children's librarians are also beginning to see that the process begins at birth and that baby's language acquisition, oral expression, and symbolic representation are all part of the process. Librarians also see the very real risk of missing this sweet spot in language development and are beginning to grasp the implication of so much lost potential. At the library, infants and toddlers are all invited to participate in expanded opportunities for engaging in the spoken word, broadening their vocabulary base, and being introduced to and stimulated by books. It is one of the best environments available to them for *active* participation in the overall early language–learning experience.

Infant and Toddler Programming

Lapsit and early toddler storytimes are appearing all over the library landscape. Along with providing programming ideas for presentation to the public, several of the newer professional publications spend considerable energy educating readers on such developmental aspects as the value of play, the processes involved in emerging literacy, and the value of providing safe public spaces for this population. This healthy trend speaks to the importance of being knowledgeable about these processes. Most librarians, however, limit their *application* of this knowledge to providing programs and should consider ways in which they can extend their new knowledge to the babies and toddlers and care providers who are mingling about the children's services area.

One of the finest examples of how librarianship has embraced and implemented current research in infant and early childhood development can be found in the area of providing quality programming. Although librarians welcome the care provider as the primary *participant* in lapsit storytimes, babies and early walkers are the primary *focus* of entertainment and enrichment, and it is in keeping with the convictions of a qualified children's librarian to provide these excellent programs. Doing so, however, is risky—and a little tricky. It is no wonder that the profession places so much emphasis on creating successful infant and baby programs. In some respects this intensity may be due to the fact that striking a balance among these little patrons, all of whom are growing so rapidly from week to week, is quite a challenge. Each and every program will be as unique as the participants—and on any particular day. No amount of planning is going to play out quite as predicted. There is no guarantee that the librarian will pull off the "successful" storytime, and for the conscientious and committed librarian, "failure" at delivering a quality storytime is just not acceptable.

Much of the planning and presentation of successful lapsit programs needs to include consideration of the personalities and emotional climate of the group. For example, if a holiday is coming up, the children may be picking up on the excitement in the air. Or families may have been cooped up in their houses because of inclement weather and are finally able to be out and about. Perhaps the cold and flu season has taken its toll. Maybe the smell of spring is in the air. Because of such circumstances, each carefully planned program will unfold in unexpected ways.

Lapsit programs are also affected by the specific group dynamics. Age ranges at this stage are going to make a big impact on the programs. Programs for participants ranging from three to six months old, along with the occasional toddler, will be very different from programs in which most of the little ones are in the twelve- to eighteen-month range. Individual temperaments also contribute to the outcome of a program. Some of the children (and caregivers) may be quite shy, or nervous, or easily frightened. There may be one very outspoken and lively child who can make or break the event. Sometimes, most of the participants are accompanied by grandparents, many of whom may be less energetic or have physical limitations. There are also issues of the day: baby didn't "get his nap"; baby and toddler may be just fine, but mommy may be exhausted and not very energetic from yet another interrupted night's sleep.

Infants are keen observers of all that is in their surroundings and can benefit just by witnessing the activities during storytime. They will study the behaviors of the other children, attend to the voice of the librarian, enjoy any music being played, and follow others' gazes, seeing for themselves what is important at the moment. They will also focus on the books being shared. Challenging as it is to plan and deliver infant and toddler programs, planning for the slightly older child may often be the best course of action. For example, the librarian may be wise to play a game of head-shoulders-knees-and-toes with active toddlers while mommy plays an adapted version with her infant instead of playing peekaboo and expecting the older children to remain engaged for very long.

The encouraging thing to remember is that, even if the program becomes completely derailed by one upset child who emotionally infects the entire group, even to the point of having to end the program, it is still a success, not only for the participants but also for the librarian. Caregivers, children, and librarians are enjoying (and sometimes commiserating with) each other; building relational bonds; learning a few new fingerplays, baby bounces, or parenting tips; making friends; and finding mutual support. So what if today's program didn't go off quite as planned? All things considered, with babies and toddlers, why would anyone think it would go perfectly smoothly in the first place? Usually the program goes much better than anticipated or predicted. The responses of the children are a source of inspiration, a great joy, amusing, and delightful. And there's always next week . . .

Librarians provide entry-level, quality, education-facilitating service to babies every day but may not recognize it as such. By encouraging the many ways in which babies are learning language and exercising their ability to communicate, librarians advance their mission of raising readers.

Baby Steps

- Purchase as many books that name and label things as you can find and actively market them to parents.
- Engage in conversation using a variety of words to assist in language acquisition.
- Invite local health departments to provide hearing and vision screening tests at the library.
- Invite local audiologists to provide a program or workshop about hearing and the acquisition of language, along with strategies for preventing and detecting hearing loss.
- Use big words, such as "excavator," "incline," or "aardvark." Babies can handle such words, they love them, and they need to hear them.
- Use puppets to tell short, outrageous, fun stories that expand vocabulary and that expose babies to the beginning-middle-end sequencing that is part of the reading process.
- Sing a little song just because, when interacting with babies, as singing provides yet another form of language learning.

Big Steps

- Gift every first-time visiting baby with a brand new board book. Physically handing the baby a book (to keep, so she can put it in her mouth if she chooses) is the very first active "readers' advisory" transaction! (This suggestion is considered a Big Step because it implies a supporting budget. However, the same message can be sent by simply handing a baby a board book from your collection, with permission from the caregiver.)

- Enlist a local service group or your Friends of the Library group to provide ongoing support for a board book distribution program.
- Provide a series of adult education classes about emerging literacy for parents and caregivers.
- Invite lecturers to speak to staff members about various components of early literacy.
- Consider learning American Sign Language and use that skill when interacting with babies and toddlers.

CARE PROVIDERS' INTELLECTUAL PURSUITS

A baby in the library implies a care provider who might also have library-related interests and information needs. However, the challenge of pursuing those interests with a baby in tow often outweighs the ability or desire to do so (see the feature "A Book for Mom?"). For example, the adult who would otherwise like to browse for books in the adult section with her toddler and infant fears being unwanted. Children are quite manageable as long as they are holding an adult hand. But let go of that hand for even a second and that little one is off like a rocket, which can be distracting to other browsers, not to mention dangerous for the child. As one parent stated, "I feel seriously unwanted in the adult section."

Of course, there are numerous ways that adults can now access titles, such as through online searches, library publications, and the like. However, it is no secret to those in the profession that serendipitous discovery of materials while browsing is very much a part of the enjoyable library experience. For parents and care providers, such discovery should also be *possible*. Perhaps it has never dawned on the parent-as-browser that books about homemade baby food, cloth diapering, or alternative discipline methods even exist. Conversely, she may want to explore subjects *not* related to parenting for a change. By becoming more aware of and sensitive to this issue, librarians can begin to brainstorm ideas and to offer solid solutions to the problem of adults with little children being denied access to library materials, even if that denial is imagined or self-imposed.

Baby Steps

- Taking a cue from the merchandising industry, purchase a few small, department store–style shopping carts with little seats that allow the caregiver to browse in adult areas while containing both infant (at the top in a carrier) and toddler (in front, strapped in). Such carts would allow the adult to go shopping, or browse, for books, videos, and periodicals in areas that are not conducive to strollers, wandering toddlers and pre-schoolers, and baby carriers.

- Create an in-house babysitting service, staffed by local preschool education students, Girl or Boy Scout groups, retired teachers, or other volunteers.
- Move some of the more pertinent periodicals of interest to parents from the periodicals room into the children's area, where they can be perused conveniently as well as chosen for checking out.
- Create a browsable section of books on the subject of parenting in the children's area.
- Advertise a valet pick-up service for parents who may have book lists but do not want to venture into the adult stacks to retrieve them. Although

A Book for Mom?

A conscientious librarian took great pains to create a display about parenting during the Mother's Day season. It enticed the mother of two young children to take a closer look, which was, after all, the intention. But the outcome was not a circulation statistic. Mom wanted to at least try to read a newly released book about making baby clothes that she saw on the display. She bravely entered the adult section toting her infant in a carrier and holding the hand of her toddler. In order to examine the back matter of the book, she put the carrier on the floor, looked at her toddler, and, in hushed tones, told him to "stay right here with Mommy." In a flash, the toddler was out of her sight, around the corner, and delightfully pulling books from the bookshelves.

Mom tossed the book down, grabbed the baby carrier, and hurried off to rescue the situation. As she made a hasty exit from the area, she could feel the glare from other patrons and even from an unsympathetic staff member. The otherwise useful information from the book didn't make it all the way to its intended reader. As a further consequence, this embarrassed mommy won't likely brave the periodicals or reading room, where the parenting magazines are kept. And you can forget about her entering the stacks! Aside from hiring a babysitter, which, in this case, she cannot afford to do, what are her alternatives? So she thinks, "I give up. I guess I don't have time to read anyway. Going to the library for myself will just have to wait." One parent interviewed said, "I pick my battles. I'm not even going anywhere near the adult section! We just stay in the children's area." These situations shouldn't be viewed as battle-zone issues. After all, it is the public library!

most librarians would be happy to fetch books for patrons, parents may feel that asking the librarian to do so would be an imposition. (First-time users with little children may feel especially self-conscious in this regard.)

- Ask your families what may be of help to them in their efforts to browse, retrieve, and check out materials. They often have great suggestions.
- Borrow a toddler and visit an unfamiliar library with the intention of browsing in the adult area. Observe your experience. Note other patrons' or staff members' responses to your visit. Invite others in your department to do the same. Share your observations.
- If a caregiver shows interest in a particular topic, say, model railroading, but does not want to attempt to leave the children's room, offer to pull that section of books from the shelf for his perusal. Putting them directly onto a book cart will allow you easier retrieval and return and will make browsing possible for the patron.
- Offer text and telephone service and arrange for curbside pickup for families who do not feel up to making a full visit to the library.
- Collaborate with adult services to offer programs for parents and caregivers specific to healthy family growth, such as making baby food, creating "organic" music, or planting edible landscaping, in which the entire family can participate.

Big Steps

- If your library is considering a large overhaul, look at ways in which collections that may be of interest to parents could be shelved nearer the children's area.
- Install a self-checkout station in the children's area.

SERVING THE INTELLECTUAL NEEDS OF FAMILIES

Children's services librarians have made great strides in providing infants and toddlers with meaningful programs geared specifically for their place on the developmental trajectory. Lapsit storytimes, summer reading programs that include incentives and programming for babies, board books, and toys in the children's area are all wonderful examples of how the profession has made adjustments to serve this population. Librarianship as a profession is embracing and defining more fully the role of librarians as education facilitators.

Valerie Gross asserts that "*everything we do* falls squarely under *education—what the world holds in highest esteem*" (italics in original).[11] If this assertion is true for the general profession, how much more so is it the case for babies who are truly learning *everything*—and *all the time?*

As a group, however, children's librarians do not tend to see themselves as providing rich intellectual experiences through casual encounters at the library. It is quite likely that they are already making contributions in these ways, but they may not fully realize the impact their efforts make on the developing baby's brain. As families become acquainted and interact with each other and with the children's librarian, they are all in equal learning territory. The children's library, thus, is a great "leveler" of learning for the community, and the children's librarian is all children's first education facilitator. Some families cannot afford tickets to the zoo. Some make just enough money per year to be disqualified for income-based assistance such as enrollment in Head Start yet cannot afford private preschool. Some may be wealthy yet lonely newcomers to the community hoping to find stimulation, interaction, and a child-care or preschool recommendation. The attentive librarian assists in orchestrating learning events and provides a welcoming place in which all families can experience enriched intellectual growth and development.

Notes

1. Alan Fogel, *Infancy: Infant, Family, and Society*, 4th ed. (Belmont: Thompson Learning, 2001), 166.
2. Christina S. Doyle, *Information Literacy in an Information Society: A Concept for the Information Age* (Syracuse, NY: ERIC Clearinghouse on Information and Technology, Syracuse University, 1994), 8.
3. Fogel, *Infancy*, 292.
4. Charles W. Snow and Cindy G. McGaha, *Infant Development* (Upper Saddle River, NJ: Prentice Hall, 2003), 146.
5. Renée Baillargeon, "The Acquisition of Physical Knowledge in Infancy: A Summary in Eight Lessons," in *Blackwell Handbook of Childhood Cognitive Development*, ed. Usha C. Goswami (Malden, MA: Blackwell, 2003), 46–83.
6. Saroj Nadkarni Ghoting and Pamela Martin-Diaz, *Storytimes for Everyone! Developing Young Children's Language and Literacy* (Chicago: ALA Editions, 2014), 7.
7. Snow and McGaha, *Infant Development*, 167.
8. Yudhijit Bhattacharjee, "Baby Brains: The First Year," *National Geographic* (January 2015), 71.
9. Ghoting and Martin-Diaz, *Storytimes for Everyone!*, 22.
10. Virginia A. Walter, *Children and Libraries: Getting It Right* (Chicago: American Library Association, 2001), 13.
11. Valerie J. Gross, *Transforming Our Image, Building Our Brand: The Education Advantage* (Santa Barbara, CA: ABC-CLIO, 2013), 7.

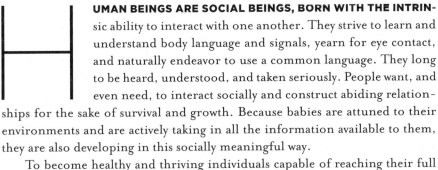

SOCIAL DEVELOPMENT
Communing with Babies
and Families

UMAN BEINGS ARE SOCIAL BEINGS, BORN WITH THE INTRIN-
sic ability to interact with one another. They strive to learn and
understand body language and signals, yearn for eye contact,
and naturally endeavor to use a common language. They long
to be heard, understood, and taken seriously. People want, and
even need, to interact socially and construct abiding relationships for the sake of survival and growth. Because babies are attuned to their
environments and are actively taking in all the information available to them,
they are also developing in this socially meaningful way.

To become healthy and thriving individuals capable of reaching their full
potential, babies *require* socialization. Research strongly supports this claim,
and just as in other areas of infant development, the healthier those social
interactions, the better for baby. It is somewhat easy to brush by this common
attribute, yet it is the primary essence of being human. An understanding of
this unfolding dynamic is an important part of providing excellent service for
babies and families.[1]

SOCIALIZATION: THE DEVELOPMENTAL TIME LINE

Babies are uniquely imbued with social powers. They have the ability to invoke
immediate responses from those in their surroundings by virtue of their cry,
laugh, gaze, pout, or smile. From birth, they construct deep, lifelong bonds

with parents, care providers, siblings, and many others with whom they come in contact. Even as these primary relationships are being built, babies are being introduced to a limited number of others in their immediate social network, such as primary care physicians, neighbors, social workers, faith-based acquaintances, and, it is hoped, children's librarians. Their social reach is somewhat limited, and their overall range of interactivity is mediated by the adult's choices and circumstances. Over time, the baby will grow into her own social network, but she comes into the world situated in her adult's unique social setting.

Over the past few decades, neuroscientists and cognitive psychologists have come to understand a great deal more about the social development of children through the first two years. Researchers are finding that children are much more sophisticated in their ability to interact with others than was anticipated. In fact, some of the social skills, especially those associated with language acquisition, are under construction even before baby is born.

From birth, the newborn recognizes his mother's voice and will respond more actively to the sounds, rhythms, and cadences of the native language he heard while in the womb. By two weeks, he recognizes his father's voice. When baby watches adult physical activity, such as hand and face movements, he will try to perform with his body what he sees, striving to imitate the movements. The newborn also has the ability to acquire any language in the world but soon attends specifically to the language of his particular culture. This language adaptation ability is powerful but fleeting. Baby will begin to focus directly on his native language, and as his brain makes the neuronal connections that support this language, he will also begin to prune out those other language inflections and tones. (One consequence of this phenomenon is that he will always be somewhat limited in his ability to communicate in the social world on a universal scale. On the other hand, this limitation allows him to focus more intensively on those within his own language base.)

By three months or so, baby is able to employ the social smile. He will beguile and entice conversation through this ability. By means of his gaze and stare, he is also able to communicate what he is feeling, what interests or bores him, or what is stimulating him. By turning his head, looking away, fussing, or crying, he is able to communicate his displeasure or discomfort. Baby is discovering that he can *create* responses from others, and he will intentionally cry or make other efforts to that end. He also recognizes that his actions cause reactions, and he delights in this newfound ability. He is learning to read faces and responds by "conversing" with pauses, similar expressions, and coos. Baby will study the adult's face with fierce concentration while making these exchanges.

By eight months, baby begins to understand that there is a social beginning, middle, and end to events. Baby knows that there are predictable patterns to chains of events and may be disconcerted if those patterns are disrupted. At this age, too, baby will begin to turn his head to follow an adult's gaze to see what is interesting. He will also focus on objects to which an adult is pointing, such as the puppy on the page of a book or, perhaps, a fish in an aquarium. Baby, too, is learning about others' intentions—he can determine the difference between someone who *cannot* offer a snack and someone who *will not* do so and can communicate his feelings regarding this knowledge.

By baby's first birthday, he is beginning to understand the difference between *accidental* and *purposeful* actions of others. He knows that some activities, such as cell phone use, are unique to humans. He also begins to understand that other people have preferences that are different from his own. He understands about fifty words, although he will not actively speak them until he is a bit older. By this age, he will demonstrate his knowledge of some of the culture's tools of communication and will correctly position a telephone (or other symbolic toy, such as a shoe) to his ear and pretend to engage in dialogue. He will eagerly and actively converse with adults, pointing and asking fledgling questions such as "Dis? Dis?" as he learns the names of things, communicates his interest, and interacts with others through his growing sophistication with language and its use.

Interestingly, by eighteen months, baby will begin to recognize himself *as* himself in a mirror. Up to this point in the infant's life, he has seen his reflected image as a separate being. Now he begins to fully see himself as a unique "other." Researchers believe it is at this point in the baby-turned-toddler's life that a true sense of consciousness begins, and the lifelong question "Who am I?" begins to emerge. This newfound awareness ushers in new social challenges, as the toddler becomes more cognizant of the individuality of others. Socializing becomes much more sophisticated as toddlers enter this stage. Up to this point, activities such as sharing, turn-taking, waiting in line, and countless other civil and cultural expectations have been introduced and encouraged on baby's part. Now, as self-awareness enters the stage, common, appropriate social behaviors are expected of him, but he must also choose to act upon them *independently* .

BABIES SOCIALIZING IN THE LIBRARY

Without a doubt, the ability to grow and engage socially is a fascinating component of the baby's development, and children's libraries have a part to play in this developmental process (see the feature "Infant Gazing"). Saroj Ghoting and Pamela Martin-Diaz state that "[t]he idea of the library as being that 'third place'—neither home nor work—where people feel comfortable socializing, and perhaps learning together, is one that many libraries are embracing."[2] Indeed, we've traditionally been that place, but perhaps never fully recognized ourselves in this way, especially where new parents, and new arrivals to the community, are concerned. Healthy social development is profoundly important, and libraries are perfectly situated to assist in this process.

Many of life's greatest joys and deepest sorrows occur within relationships. After all, the ability to forge friendships, build intimate bonds, express love and compassion, provide comfort and empathy, and share laughter and pain is what makes humans so very special. (Indeed, there are some who contend that the decline of social interactivity experienced during play coincides with the cultural rise in psychopathology in children.) Baby is learning how to grow into these meaningful relationships from the very first days of life and will continue to be strongly influenced by them until his very last.[3]

As adults, it is tempting to trivialize social encounters as secondary to quality service. This just isn't so. As librarians recognize the value of the developing social life of the baby, they can also take proactive steps to assist in that process.

Baby Steps

- Greet your youngest patrons (and caregivers) by name. Fully making eye contact may require moving out from behind the desk and going to them, because babies might be in carriers or wrapped up in their mother's arms.

Infant Gazing

Infants gaze, and with great intensity. And they are especially drawn to and are inherently interested in faces. After all, faces are highly expressive and animated. These two phenomena work together to create deep connections between infants and their primary caregivers. Through this mutual interaction, they become exquisitely responsive to each other. This developmental process ushers in social interactions such as babbling and smiling. From as early as three months, babies control where they look, what they look at, and for how long. As one researcher states, gazing interactions are not a preliminary to something else; rather, "[t]hey are that something. He cannot reach, or give, or take, or point, or show, or ask, or comment upon anything. He is caught in this rich and intense world of the nonverbal, the purely interpersonal, the immediate. He is captured there by design and default, at least until about six months of age."*

Further, "[a baby's] only 'topic' is the single moment happening now: two human beings mutually engaged."† The ability to gaze is a major and integral part of the process of building the baseline brain infrastructure for engaging in future social interactions. Taken to its logical next step, the primary means by which a librarian can fully interact with and truly "listen" to the infant, mindful of this developmental ability and social acuity, is to make the effort to fully engage with baby, face-to-face, in a mutual gaze.

* Daniel N. Stern, *Diary of a Baby* (New York: Basic Books, 1990), 52.
† Ibid., 51.

- Invite or otherwise create situations in which introductions can be made so that everyone learns everyone else's name.
- Create sticker name tags to assist in learning names.
- Make an effort to truly gaze into the infant's eyes, inviting this intensely social, crucial, and exclusive activity.
- Provide a collection of board books that celebrate social and cultural diversity in all of its splendor and color so baby can find a representation of herself on the printed page.
- Talk to baby, sing him a jingle, recite a little poem, and otherwise engage in language-building conversation.
- Create open-ended play opportunities in a small corner of the children's area that encourage social interactions and that are available whenever the library doors are open.
- Structure and advertise play dates to provide occasions for families to meet one another in a more casual and noncommittal fashion.
- Engage with babies and care providers socially during their visit, within reason, because the gesture is not only welcoming but also developmentally valuable.
- Take a walkabout and seek out baby while she is waiting for her adult to attend to tasks, taking a minute or two to reconnect with baby.
- Make small incentives routinely available; stickers or hand stamps are great means of enticement and regular interaction.

Big Step

- Create an advertising campaign emphasizing the library as an institution specifically suited to fostering healthy social development.

BABIES ENGAGING WITH OTHERS

Babies and toddlers are exquisitely designed to absorb their sociocultural worlds and the nonverbal messages of social interaction. They are continually attuned to the ongoing exchanges that are being made, especially within the give-and-take of the care provider's interaction with baby. But care providers aren't the only ones interacting with babies in the library. Baby is also being introduced to the many and diverse "others" outside his immediate social unit. As one of the first public institutions that infants and toddlers encounter, the library "help[s] children to mediate between their private lives and the more public roles in their community."[4]

Baby to Baby

When baby visits the children's area of the library, she is likely to encounter other babies and children. Babies and toddlers love to be around other babies and children. For many very young children, the library is one of the few places where they can come into contact with each other. For the most part, being around other babies usually is (or at least should be) a happy, playful, enjoyable event, if the babies have an adequate place to move about and get acquainted in their own little ways (see the feature "Bouncing Baby George Finds a Friend"). Babies, given the opportunity, will gravitate toward each other and actively attempt to reach out to make physical contact. When given a place in which to do so, babies and toddlers can be quite active in this way. They are also learning how to interact with the various temperaments and mannerisms of others. Even one-time encounters are beneficial, but regular contact is better.

Lapsit programs, to some degree, are designed to allow for these baby-to-baby interactions and can be quite successful in this regard. However, babies should also be able to socialize in the general children's area, as many babies will never have the opportunity to attend structured programs. Babies shouldn't need to wait until they are older to begin making the social connections that further relationships. Babies who serendipitously meet in the library will be of similar

Bouncing Baby George Finds a Friend

Eight-month-old George was visiting the library with his mother. Mother had taken George out of the stroller and plopped him down in the infant play area near the mirror. It wasn't long before George caught sight of himself and, with all the enthusiasm he could muster, began to do a full-body bounce on his bottom, arms flailing, face beaming with delight at the activity of that "other" baby. When his mother spoke, off to the left, George halted his bouncing and turned his head in her direction, distracted by her speech sounds. Soon, however, in his peripheral vision, George caught a glimpse of "that baby" in the mirror and again vigorously began the delightful bouncing exchange. This very physical activity went on for a full fifteen minutes! Baby George played with his "friend" in the mirror at the library and, judging by the gleeful look on his face, had a wonderful experience. The observing librarian was astonished at George's attention span, his physical stamina, and his keen awareness of his "playmate." George didn't make many vocalizations, and it would have been easy to miss what was really transpiring. George was actively—very actively—advancing his social skills in his safe play with his little "friend" at the library.

age. It isn't unreasonable to think that these early contacts may grow to become friendships and the others become first dates, teammates, or classmates. The children can then honestly say that they "knew each other when" and that they first met at the public library. Thus, librarians become instrumental in making these lifelong associations possible at a much earlier time in children's lives, giving them the chance to forge deep relationships indeed.

Baby to Adult

By necessity, baby comes to the library with a care provider. This care provider is often actively involved in assisting the little one to learn some of the social graces. Mild admonishments such as "No, no, baby mustn't grab for his hair," or "It's her turn so you have to wait," or "Be gentle" are often overheard. These and countless other promptings are all geared toward teaching the baby and toddler how to be socially responsible and are meant to instill early messages of consideration and compassion. Even as baby is learning what sound a cow makes, which crayon is the red one, or whether the ball will yet again obey the laws of gravity, he is also learning to *socialize* in *society*. Ghoting and Martin-Diaz state that "[y]oung children learn best when they are building on what they know, when adults build on their interests, and when they are exposed to new facts and ideas *in a social context*" (emphasis added).[5]

Baby is busy observing the ways in which adults interact with one another and learning that her care provider may be different from other adults. These social others may display differing communication styles, skin color, or ethnic dress. They may represent a different gender or generation. At the library, babies are encountering these larger sociocultural worlds under somewhat manageable circumstances. And baby is concurrently receiving the message, by way of the general context of library philosophy, that all are welcome and are to be respected.

Another side of this socialization discussion also must be addressed, as most librarians can sadly attest. Some babies come to the library with insensitive adults and are sometimes flatly ignored or disregarded as the adult preoccupies herself with the Internet, the latest best seller, or the selection of horror DVDs. The public is, after all, the public, and not everyone carries the same level of conviction regarding what is in the best interests of the baby or toddler. And as long as this difference of convictions does not blatantly harm the child, it is not the librarian's responsibility to challenge it.

Of course, the subject of differences of opinion regarding child-rearing philosophies is decidedly gray and requires the finesse of a trapeze artist to navigate. Some adults are quite tolerant of their children, almost to the point of indifference. Others are very strict, keeping close tabs on all baby activity, quick to point out any errors. Some communicate and discipline in covert ways, while others are outspoken and harsh. One very useful solution to this problem is for the library to offer appropriate play areas that allow the indifferent adult to pursue her library interests while her toddler plays nearby. The benefits are numerous and well worth the investment for the good of everyone. First, the adult, who would otherwise be parked at an adult computer workstation with, basically, an unattended child, can be redirected to a better situation, much to the relief of both adult services staff and patrons. Second, devoting space for adults in this way makes it somewhat easier and gentler to direct the adult's attention to the behavior of her child as needed, as they are in proximity.

In addition, in this more comprehensive environment, a little one might benefit from watching others interact in healthier and more socially appropriate ways. An otherwise ignored toddler may even be invited to play and converse with other caring adults, especially as he begins to move about more independently. Interacting with the children's librarian offers yet another positive social exchange. Finally, by interacting in an appropriate space in which babies and adults are grouped together, the otherwise preoccupied (or overly occupied) adult may also witness healthier alternatives and begin to adapt her own philosophy of parenting.

ENCOURAGING BABY SOCIAL EXCHANGE

Overall healthy development requires that baby engage in positive social activity. What better place than in the children's department of the local library? It really doesn't require much more than an investment of time.

Baby Steps

- Promote pre-literacy skills by allowing baby and toddler patrons to create their own name tags in their own indecipherable way.
- Enter into the play experience with babies and families.
- Offer coloring pages or make-it-take-it crafts that invite sharing activity and turn-taking for the very young, using glue sticks, crayons, markers, or stamp pads.
- Blow bubbles together.
- Spontaneously share a sing-along story or book.
- Create a collection of special toys or novelty books that you can use to spark curiosity, conversation, and interaction.
- Install a shatter-proof mirror somewhere in the baby's line of vision for self-exploration and discovery.

Big Step

- Dedicate more staff hours and funding for the specific purpose of serving babies in more impromptu ways rather than limiting social exchanges to structured programs.

BABIES ENGAGING WITH LIBRARIANS, BOOKS, AND AUTHORS

The most important social interaction baby can make while at the library, of course, is meeting and building a relationship with his librarian. After all, this relationship is one of the primary factors that identifies the library as a social institution. As a rule, librarians are aware of this aspect of the library experience but really don't give it much thought. However, the opportunity to be a relationship builder carries with it great potential. For instance, when a librarian offers a smile to baby and caregiver and that smile is acknowledged, a social interaction has just been established, thus opening the door for further social interactions. A warm hello and other words of welcome begin the verbal conversation and the building of trust among all three parties. These are primary steps that need to be made before making a book recommendation. As the librarian takes the time to approach baby or otherwise engage baby's gaze, baby and his librarian enjoy a few one-on-one moments with each other, *outside* baby's relationship with his care provider. Over time, this relationship can grow to become a friendship, and the librarian can become one of baby's trusted adults outside the family unit.

Because baby is dependent upon the direct social interactions of adults, *it is up to the librarian* to make the first move, because baby cannot. This initial welcoming encounter may be especially important if the care provider is new to library culture, feels out of his element, is shy or uncertain, or in other ways is not likely to approach the librarian or to introduce baby. Further, as the librarian presents baby with a book, she is also introducing the rich tradition of her profession—making a book recommendation. She is actively planting the first seeds for fostering a love of reading. And she is demonstrating to the attending adult that librarians champion reading and provide information for the children in their community and that such service is fully extended to babies, toddlers, and care providers.

Through the conveyance of books, baby is introduced to an entirely new neighborhood. It is a vast and wonderful place full of stories, pictures, animals, imagination, language, science, poetry, and all the other aspects books have to offer. The book as an object, however, ultimately represents the person (author or illustrator) who wrote it in an effort to *communicate*. Writers, of course, express thoughts, feelings, facts, and other forms of information in the hope of being read, heard, interpreted, understood, and perhaps even shared. Some of these authors and illustrators create books just for babies. Their intent is to participate with babies in the social world they hold in common.

Writers for babies may discuss various household objects or events, states of weather, body parts, or emotional expressions. They may name the animals in a barnyard, introduce baby to jungle animals, or invite baby to seek-and-find. Through the medium of the book, author and baby are sharing in the literacy-based event of social interaction and communication. Playing with, perusing, or otherwise sharing books can thus be understood, and maybe even *best* understood, as a social event. Baby is also quite capable of choosing favorites and gravitating in very physical ways to the author or illustrator that speaks to him. After all, even as baby delights in the pages of a book, he is interacting with print designed to speak to him even as his brain is prolifically making connections. Hence, as librarians strive to promote books and to encourage pre- and early literacy skills, they are ultimately attempting to make introductions into this vast social network. Moreover, as baby, author, illustrator, mommy, sibling, and librarian share books together, they are *engaging in community* in the best possible sense.

Because of the intense, whole-brain learning experience in which babies and toddlers are engaged, interacting with authors through books may well be the most influential and literacy-rich activity in their lives.

Baby Steps

- Spread out an assortment of books for baby to see, reach for, choose, and touch.
- Build collections for baby to peruse that represent social interactions, diversity, and family dynamics.
- Spontaneously engage in a book, or even just a page of a book, with baby, attending to her temperament, attention span, interaction skills, and developmental level.
- Share a quick book or two with a small group of babies as they serendipitously meet at the library, inviting and including siblings.
- Encourage preschool-age siblings to share books with baby brother or sister.
- Spontaneously engage a small group of babies in a fingerplay, song, or chant.
- Purchase a few sturdy, child-sized shopping carts for early walkers to use to practice walking, socializing, and selecting books. Because books are heavy and huge in a baby's arms or hands, this is a great method of allowing baby and adult to gather today's selections.

Big Steps

- Create and maintain a noncirculating collection of board books that are more interactive, such as books that are embedded with puppets, flaps, and spinner toys.
- Purchase a stock of mildly interactive board books as giveaways to first-time library visitors, equating books with the library and librarianship.

CARE PROVIDERS SOCIALIZING IN THE LIBRARY

Babies, of course, do not come to the library alone. They come with new mothers, newcomers to the community, overtaxed and overtired parents, grandparents, or teen sibling babysitters, and often with a toddler or preschooler. All these companions have their own social needs and agendas. Some just want to get out of the house. Some come because they know of no other safe place to go. Some enter the library because it is free to do so. For whatever reason they are there, they typically anticipate a social encounter, however small it may be. Care providers of very young children are often socially isolated and genuinely seek out encounters with other people. For some of these patrons, being in the library gives them a chance to just take a break. As baby and toddler are preoccupied in the fresh yet gentle stimulation of library play, the adult can relax a bit. After all, caring for little ones is an around-the-clock responsibility.

Adult to Adult

When visiting the library, many child-care providers find that there are other adults dealing with similar joys and challenges. Even as relative strangers, mothers, fathers, and other care providers commiserate over lost sleep and the cost of disposable diapers. They share tips on how to manage whining, teething, and impulsive biting. They introduce each other's children and appreciate the babies' collective adorability. They also swap recipes, coupons, websites, experiences, and other bits of information, usually happy to share what they've come to know. They share stories, anecdotes, pictures, and invitations. Serendipitous meetings at the library can sometimes result in friendships being established and play dates arranged.

Adults often meet, become acquainted, and even become friends with other adults through the activity of their children, whether it is from sitting near each other on the school bleachers, attending Scout meetings in a church fellowship hall, or waiting for band practice to end. The library, as one of the few public places where families of very young children may congregate, provides a place in which to make connections and build that social network at a much earlier time, whether by chance meetings or through structured infant and toddler programs. The public library, therefore, provides a safe, logical first destination for fostering healthy social encounters for these families.

Adult to Baby

Of course, one of the social interactions librarians encourage is the involvement of the adult with her infant or toddler. Libraries foster this type of interaction regularly through programming and by providing simple toys, puzzles, and books. Learning through play is, of course, the way in which babies are understanding the world. *Active* participation on the part of the adult is necessary for success in any learning process. Such participation includes the encouraging, coaching, modeling, and guiding of baby's social development and interactions.

Adult care providers' sharing of books with babies is one of the primary social encounters librarians want to encourage. Yes, this practice promotes reading and pre-reading skills. But much more is happening. As Ghoting and Martin-Diaz point out, "[c]hildren who are read to early and often succeed not just because they are exposed to books, but also because the experience of sharing books with adults reflects their *engagement* in the process, the particular strategies of parent and other adults, and children's *interpersonal relationships* with adults" (emphasis added).[6] These are, quite obviously, *social* events. Sharing books is a wonderful means of supporting and advancing social exchanges. Furthermore, for some adults, sharing board books or reading stories together works when other forms of interaction or communication are less successful. Some adults are ill-equipped or inexperienced when it comes to engaging in developmentally appropriate conversations with a baby or toddler. Books are a means of bridging that gap as they focus both parties' attention on the printed page where they mutually share in the content and dialogue about what they see.

Another social dynamic that arises from visits to the library involves the interactions of adults with other babies. As parents and care providers interact, they begin to learn about and become more familiar with babies who are quite different from their own. Perhaps one baby is more outspoken, another is more curious, and still another exhibits extreme shyness. These various meetings provide some adults with opportunities to better understand that every baby is unique and quite different from every other. Over time, the relationships that have begun in the library may continue to play out in the larger world. Libraries in smaller communities are especially likely to introduce adults to others' children, who will quite possibly cross paths numerous times over their developing years. As one parent stated, "I have a pretty good understanding of how these kids may develop as a group over the years, just by seeing how they interact even now! I'm also glad to know which ones tend to be a bit shy, may be instigators, in a good way, which ones to watch out for, and which kid may turn out to be a bully."

ENCOURAGING ADULT SOCIAL EXCHANGE

In the past, libraries discouraged adults from being active participants in the children's area. Thankfully, that approach has changed as librarians and parents have joined forces, working together toward the common goal of fostering healthy growth, which includes the development of good social skills.

Baby Steps

- Make introductions whenever possible, especially of yourself.
- Advertise an open invitation to a play date at the library for families with babies.
- Hold an open house for new parents.
- Use social media sites as places for care providers to connect with others and with the library in the virtual world.
- Arrange seating so that adults can socialize with each other while observing their children at play.
- Create programs, such as cooking or crafting classes, that encourage adult-to-adult interactions and that include babies.
- Start conversations with small groups of care providers, and then let them talk.

Big Steps

- Create cuddly reading corners and nooks that invite togetherness.
- Purchase an extra-wide chair or two so baby, mommy, and toddler can all sit and read together.
- Provide some portable seating that adults can rearrange so they can gather in small groups.

CARE PROVIDERS ENGAGING WITH LIBRARIANS, BOOKS, AND AUTHORS

Of course, adults with babies also interact with librarians. This is one area of providing service to babies in which a librarian can truly shine. Many adults with babies and toddlers are coming to the library because "it is the right thing to do," but they may not have a clue about *why*. They may not be familiar with the various collections housed in the children's area, or they may be quite reluctant to seek out the librarian, not knowing what a librarian *does*, let alone how she could be of service.

Adult to Children's Librarian

Adults new to the children's library can sometimes feel a bit lost and may easily become overwhelmed as they learn about all the resources available to them and their children. They may have no idea that the library holds a huge collection of children's music that includes lullabies and educational content for babies. Some do not know that there are magazines published for very young children or that the local library collects and circulates toys or other educational media for infants and toddlers. Most, but not all, adults are aware of board books but do not necessarily know that such items can be checked out.

Care providers may not even be aware that there are programs that are structured and offered specifically for babies. Further, as parents continue to engage in the types of social and educational opportunities provided by interactive media, they may need guidance on how best to use their handheld devices for their children's enrichment. This awareness is especially important with respect to striving for a healthy balance of device-interactive and non-technological forms of play with their babies. The children's librarian has the distinct pleasure and responsibility of being available to introduce these various collections and resources and to offer suggestions for their application, function, or use.[7]

Some adults may be experiencing the social isolation that having a baby can sometimes bring and are lonely and just want to chat. Although a balancing act is required, a certain amount of interaction between the librarian and the somewhat needful adult may be necessary. Some care providers, such as new mothers or fathers, may be very vulnerable and unsure of themselves and have no idea what a children's library is all about as a public institution. Some may have had numerous encounters with social services providers or others who have treated them with disdain, condescension, or deprecation and may be wary of the approach and offer of services by the public librarian.

It is in this somewhat delicate social framework that the professional librarian can truly make a positive impact. As relationships are established and confidentiality maintained, mutual respect and trust have a chance to grow. Having a friend in the children's area where everyone is welcome can be a huge source of comfort, support, and relief. Children's librarians can, and often do, serve these patrons in small yet powerful and life-changing ways just by offering a kind word or gesture. Serving patrons in this manner, however, can be easily overlooked or perceived as trivial.

Through the building and nurturing of positive relationships, the librarian's book recommendations, offers of information, or referrals to service agencies are more likely to be interpreted as extensions of caring service, not as pedantic messages delivered with undertones of accusation or judgment. With repeat visits, the children's librarian becomes a liaison and friend to the family. Many librarians know the interactions well, as they hear about situations that would benefit from intervention or information, and then gently make referrals in this regard. The first step in making these recommendations, however, is the establishment of relationships.

Adult to Children's Authors

Introducing new parents and care providers to the vast holdings of the children's section in the library is a wonderful part of being a children's librarian (see the feature "New Parents Meet Children's Services"). Inviting a parent or care provider to become better acquainted with the rich repertoire of children's literature, music, toy collections, and other materials is quite gratifying. New parents may be familiar with long-standing classic children's books but quite unaware of the many works for babies and toddlers. Some are still afraid that baby will "tear up a book," unaware of the board books marketed specifically for babies. *Many* adults are unaware of nonfiction books in which simple content, vivid color, and striking illustrations are of keen interest to babies and toddlers. Also, books that name things, such as those that introduce baby to, say, the first hundred words on the farm, as well as classic nursery rhyme books are often published in standard hardback form and are of great interest to the care provider. It is the librarian's unique privilege to connect adults with these books and authors. Usually the adult will come away from these first encounters somewhat overwhelmed but giddy with excitement, hardly knowing where to begin. For some, it may mean acquiring their very first library card—ever.

ENCOURAGING SOCIAL EXCHANGE BETWEEN CARE PROVIDER AND CHILDREN'S LIBRARIAN

Social interactions take time. Of course, time constraints are already a huge challenge for children's librarians. Nevertheless, the potential these exchanges carry justifies their inclusion in providing quality library service.

Baby Steps

- Taking cues from successful businesses, ask your patrons if you can be of assistance. Although they may pass on the invitation, they are made aware that their presence has been noted and acknowledged.
- Get to know families, because doing so is very much a part of service to them.

New Parents Meet Children's Services

One morning, a children's librarian looked up from her desk and noticed a couple at the circulation desk toting a baby carrier. Because she did not recognize them, she decided to take a minute to introduce herself. As it turned out, the couple was quite familiar with the video section of the library and were making their first visit for videos since the birth of their son three weeks ago. As introductions were made, the librarian asked them if they wanted to hear more about what the children's library had to offer their baby. They glanced unenthusiastically at each other but decided to hear her out. Mildly curious at best, and obviously skeptical, they politely and rather dutifully followed her to the children's area. The librarian showed them where the board books were kept and where the play area was located and told them about the nursery rhyme and nonfiction books. She showed them the nursing area and pointed out the corner in which community support and parent information was kept.

The librarian also invited the couple to use the adult computer in the children's area as needed, so they would feel more comfortable if the baby should cry or otherwise make noise. She told them about videos, toys, and other items available to their son as he grew. She really got their attention when she told them about the lullaby collection that was inspired by heavy metal bands! She invited them to attend lapsit storytimes and to feel free to just hang out whenever they needed a break from home.

The somewhat awed look on the mother's face was priceless. She looked around rather slowly with obvious information overload and finally mused, "Honestly, I had no idea. . . . Wow." Meanwhile, dad was busily ruffling through the music offerings, smiling with both amazement and amusement on his face. They expressed their sincere gratitude and spent a little time milling about the area. Since then, they have become regular visitors to the children's department, although they were reluctant to commit to attending structured storytimes. Their son, now just past his first birthday, knows and smiles at his very own librarian and obviously enjoys the time he spends in the library. The family has made many acquaintances and is frequently seen engaged in play. This little success story all began with a librarian noticing a new baby, taking the time to make a simple introduction, and extending an invitation to become better acquainted.

- Celebrate monthly birthdays up to twenty-four months by having special stickers devoted to just this purpose. This practice not only acknowledges the rapid rate at which children are growing and developing but also furthers social interactions and affirmations.
- Introduce and celebrate the board book "author of the month" for adults, so they become more familiar with the collection from the librarian's point of view.
- Make comprehensive displays of books, music, media, and other items that are baby-oriented but perhaps unknown to adults, such as lullabies, sign language, and Mother Goose.
- Advertise an "app of the month" and other educational sites for handheld interactive devices.
- Create a handout or brochure of helpful apps and websites that can be spontaneously offered as educational supports for parent-and-baby device interactions.

Big Steps

- Armed with research and statistics regarding this population and the importance of spending spontaneous time together, approach human resources and administration for more funding and staff hours.
- Take a long, hard look at how professional time is being spent and determine whether some of the practices currently in place could be changed, altered, or even eliminated in order to make more time and resources available for families with babies and toddlers.

LIBRARIANS AS SOCIAL CONVENERS

Children's librarians have the opportunity to be participants in the important task of fostering social development. By providing a unique place for encouraging social encounters, and by fostering positive relationships, librarians are assisting in setting the stage for all future interactions, including the very important connection of person-to-author. Virginia Walter, in *Children and Libraries: Getting It Right,* offers the following invitation: "If the library fulfills this mediating function successfully, it can facilitate access to the books and information children need to thrive. It can also nurture their overall development as productive members of society. When libraries see their young patrons as part of a community, they are likely to serve them holistically."[8] These words capture so beautifully the impact that the library can make on *all* children, including, of course, babies and toddlers, as social beings. It also serves as a reminder that babies are, indeed, holistic beings developing in physical, emotional, intellectual, and social ways.

As babies, toddlers, and care providers visit the library regularly during these first years, and as the librarian makes an effort to interact with them, the little ones are exposed to a manageable yet slightly broader social world. As their developing young brains are forging connections, healthy interactions within the library become an integral part of their social framework in very literal ways. Children's librarians, as participants in local professional communities and initial social servants, have the opportunity to make meaningful contributions to this remarkable brain growth that gently blossoms into rich and healthy relationships—a powerful calling indeed.

Notes

1. Yudhijit Bhattacharjee, "Baby Brains: The First Year," *National Geographic* (January 2015), 57–77.

2. Saroj Nadkarni Ghoting and Pamela Martin-Diaz, *Storytimes for Everyone! Developing Young Children's Language and Literacy* (Chicago: ALA Editions, 2014), xi.

3. Peter Gray, "The Decline of Play and the Rise of Psychopathology in Children and Adolescents," *American Journal of Play* 3, no. 4 (2011), 443–63.

4. Virginia A. Walter, *Children and Libraries: Getting It Right* (Chicago: American Library Association, 2001), 104.

5. Ghoting and Martin-Diaz, *Storytimes for Everyone!*, 23.

6. Ibid., 20.

7. Cen Campbell, Claudia Haines, Amy Koester, and Dorothy Stoltz, "Media Mentorship in Libraries Serving Youth," Association for Library Service to Children (2015), www.ala.org/alsc/sites/ala.org.alsc/files/content/2015%20ALSC%20White%20Paper_FINAL.pdf.

8. Walter, *Children and Libraries*, 104.

THE POTENTIAL OF LIBRARIANSHIP FOR BABIES AND FAMILIES

DELIVERING QUALITY SERVICE TO BABIES, TODDLERS, AND families requires not only the materials of library collections, and librarians to assist in acquiring them, but also the spaces in which to gather, belong, and "do." Upholding the various requirements of all the patrons who use the children's library is an enormous undertaking—overwhelming, even. Babies, toddlers, and care providers are only one set of many different populations served by children's librarians. Nevertheless, baby brain research has galvanized the profession to try to do more, and it has. Librarians are now beginning to realize that the impact they make on a baby's development has the potential to influence his developing brain for a lifetime. They are striving to provide whatever it takes to make these early years happy and positive ones, but there are more ways in which to do so. As the previous discussions begin to illuminate, the stakes here are really, *really* high. After all, these are human lives growing and developing very quickly.

There are so many sociocultural issues impacting these little ones that providing public library service for them needs to be taken seriously. Serving infants, toddlers, and their caregivers is a very complex and serious yet delightful process but ultimately simple in its delivery. The problem is that quality service takes time, even if only in bits and pieces. And time is a resource of which no librarian can possibly have enough. It isn't enough to devote time just to programming, although programs for babies and toddlers are very valuable. Quality service also requires the availability to engage in spontaneous encounters with drop-in

visitors. And, if it is to be truly successful, quality service requires the understanding and support of administration not only in hiring wisely but also in
advocating for and maintaining a level of respect toward children's librarians
and the patrons they serve.

WHERE WE HAVE BEEN, AND WHAT WE HAVE COME TO BELIEVE

Reviewing some of the tenets so deeply held by library professionals, in the
context of what research is revealing about the developing infant, gives fresh
significance to librarians' expressed convictions. A fresh reading of the tenets,
combined with research findings, provides children's librarians with solid reasons why support and funding should be made readily available so that essential
changes can be addressed. It is hoped that this brief overview will also inspire
continued discussion and dialogue among library professionals in their efforts
to better grasp the glaring need and the big picture that serving the developing
infant signifies.

The Library Bill of Rights

One of the most important documents of the profession is the American Library
Association's *Library Bill of Rights*. Article V states that "[a] person's right to use a
library should not be denied or abridged because of origin, age, background, or
views." The inclusion of "age" in this policy deserves further thought. It challenges libraries to consider how they may be denying or abridging an infant's
or toddler's *access* to materials, however innocently. If a baby or toddler cannot
safely avail herself, of her own volition, of books published specifically for her,
the library is in danger of violating this right. It is tempting to want to justify
the denial of this access with "yes, but . . ." excuses. After all, they're just babies,
right? Maybe that type of thinking is in error. This issue was revisited several
times over the years, and it was continually agreed that the inclusion of "age"
was a concept worth embracing.

　　According to the *Intellectual Freedom Manual*, the word "age" was first adopted in
a revision of the *Library Bill of Rights* in 1967. In 1980, after careful deliberation,
the word was once again confirmed and approved. The issue was visited yet
again in 1996, at which time "[t]he ALTA [Association for Library Trustees and
Advocates] brought a request to the Council to reaffirm the inclusion of 'age.'
The motion was passed by the ALA [American Library Association] Council on
January 24, 1996, *by acclamation*" (emphasis added).[1]

There can be no doubt that ALA is quite sincere about this issue, and individual libraries, at the very least, should consider how this tenet may be extended to babies and toddlers with respect to their developmental abilities and limitations. More specifically, the library itself as a place that welcomes babies and care providers should therefore make attempts to adapt *spaces* accordingly, so baby, just like everyone else, can get to her books "all by myself."

Ranganathan and the "Five Laws of Librarianship"

Another tenet commonly embraced by librarians is the Five Laws of Librarianship. These laws were first put forth by Shiyali Ramamrita Ranganathan in 1931 as a theory on how to operate a library system in India and have been adopted internationally by many libraries and librarians as the foundation of libraries' general philosophy. Revisiting these tenets with an emphasis on babies and toddlers invites a new way of considering these laws. The five laws are as follows:

1. Books are for use.
2. Every reader his book.
3. Every book its reader.
4. Save the time of the User.
5. The library is a growing organism.[2]

The first law indicates that books are for use. In Ranganathan's day, there were no board books. Today, there is a thriving industry devoted to the creation and dissemination of books for babies and toddlers.

The second law asks the librarian to consider the reader himself. Within collections of board books are individual titles, of which babies are quite capable of choosing favorites. One baby or toddler may prefer a blue book, another a red one, and yet another, a book with more subdued colors.

The third law emphasizes the books themselves. Board books are created with certain themes, subjects, or interactive elements that offer variety to individual babies and toddlers. Some books contain tabs and flaps, others may include puppets, and still others may incorporate tactile elements, all designed for the right reader. Demand for these books continues to grow among the public in general and among libraries in particular. The books' evolving inclusion of clever attributes speaks to the publishers' willingness to satisfy the pre-literacy interests and needs of developing babies.

The fourth law introduces the issue of time. It would be in baby's or toddler's best interest to *spend* time in the library. This type of activity provides baby with various forms of sensory stimulation. It exposes babies to an expanded range of ideas and experiences. It also introduces the authors themselves, represented by their books. Engaging with a book, a toy, a care provider, a sibling, another baby, or a librarian, slowing down and enjoying being in the moment, is an opportunity for baby to enjoy a library-initiated learning event.

Finally, the fifth law describes the library as a growing and changing organism. So are babies and toddlers in their very rapid way. Together, babies, toddlers, and the librarians who represent this institution have the lifelong opportunity to grow, to adapt, and to forge community relationships.

Crawford and Gorman's Revision of the "Five Laws of Librarianship"

In *Future Libraries: Dreams, Madness, and Reality*, Walt Crawford and Michael Gorman offer an updated interpretation of Ranganathan's Laws. Their revision reflects the social, cultural, and institutional changes that have transpired in libraries since Ranganathan's original laws were first published. And the revised laws also deserve a closer look with regard to their application to babies and toddlers.[3]

1. Libraries serve humanity.
2. Respect all forms by which knowledge is communicated.
3. Use technology intelligently to enhance service.
4. Protect free access to knowledge.
5. Honor the past and create the future.

The first law, of course, implies that libraries include services to babies and toddlers. Although there is nothing surprising about this conclusion, it still deserves mention because, as these discussions bear out, babies and toddlers are easily overlooked and currently are not being served equitably.

Within the library setting, the second law may require a broader interpretation to allow for the ways in which babies are acquiring and assimilating knowledge and information from the people with which they are surrounded and the places and contexts in which they find themselves. Libraries choosing to abide by this law should want to make every effort to create appropriate environments for exercising these methods of acquiring information. This law may also encourage librarians to learn about as well as better understand and respect how babies and toddlers attempt to communicate.

The third law discusses the use of technology. In the case of babies and toddlers, intelligent use of technology may also mean its de-emphasis, as deemed wise and necessary with regard to their developing needs. The overall culture is facing ongoing technological bombardment. Escaping that barrage can be calming and beneficial to everyone, especially to easily overstimulated, developing babies. They should be provided with, and encouraged to pursue, traditional, organic forms of learning through play and interactivity, more in keeping with their ability to assimilate their immediate environments. Enhanced service for this population with regard to technology may also mean equipping the play environment in a way that allows access to technology, within reason, by the adult care provider.

The fourth law challenges the library to make necessary changes to library spaces in order to first provide and then protect the means by which babies and toddlers learn and their ability to approach books independently, with consideration given to their physical skill and volition.

And finally, it is in keeping with the urgent mission of library foremothers as advocates for children to accept and include babies and toddlers in the public library. As research continues to illuminate our understanding of child development, children's librarianship is compelled to adapt services accordingly, including a careful reevaluation of the profession along with the reappointing of interior spaces.

VIRGINIA WALTER AND THE "FIVE LAWS OF CHILDREN'S LIBRARIANSHIP"

At the turn of the century, Virginia Walter, in her heartfelt book *Children and Libraries: Getting It Right,* presented her Five Laws of Children's Librarianship, based on Ranganathan's original tenets. She offered the laws in an effort "[t]o help those future children's librarians think about their vocation."[4] By examining these laws with respect to babies and toddlers, and in light of what research has now begun to reveal on their behalf, we see that these laws take on even deeper and more nuanced application.

Laws of Babies' and Toddlers' Librarianship

- Libraries serve the reading interests and information needs of all children, directly and through service to parents and other adults who are involved with the lives of children.
- Children's librarians provide the right book or information for the right child at the right time in the right place.
- Children's librarians are advocates for children's access to books, information, information technology, and ideas.
- Children's librarians promote children's literacy in all media.
- Children's librarians honor their traditions and create the future.

WHERE WE ARE AS LIBRARIANS TO BABIES AND TODDLERS

Much is expected of today's children's librarians. Children's librarians are to be quality administrators, entertainers, event planners, outreach providers, advocates across many platforms, child development specialists for birth through age whenever, liaisons to schools, early literacy coaches, media mentors, toddler-language interpreters, homework helpers, after-school caregivers, bibliographic instructors, Band-Aid providers, *and* readers' advisors and collection developers—for every child (as well as many of the adults) in the community. For some librarians, this is indeed the everyday workload. What other vocation, except perhaps parenthood, expects such a wide range of skills and abilities? Yet, as many librarians can attest, they are serving in this capacity as an army of one or two. How unrealistic. And exhausting.

Further, without adequate support, this overwhelming list of efforts made and energies spent runs the risk of being, or at the very least *feeling*, futile.

Children's Libraries Are Community Places

C hildren's librarians have been championing the cause of children in libraries for a long time, and, as a result, this service model is now deeply woven into the fabric of the institution. However, we now know and understand so much more about how babies learn and grow. Because of this flood of new research, the time has come for libraries to seriously reconsider library interiors. It is indeed possible to create a small area for babies within existing children's libraries by implementing creative space planning.

Just as libraries are embracing the creation of teen spaces, suitable safe places for gentle play for babies, toddlers, and preschoolers are also valid, along with developmentally appropriate areas for children in the early and upper elementary grades. These loosely defined groups and their complementary environments are mirrored in the structuring of our public schools. Each group, generally speaking, is learning and maturing in different major stages. Providing adequate areas for them would not only impel them away from areas that are inappropriate and, to the growing child, uninteresting but also prove relevant for the next phase of growth. As Walter states, "[i]t is unreasonable to expect that the same facility or section of a building would be appropriate for children from infancy through elementary or middle school."* Unreasonable indeed, but it is the common scenario within children's departments in public libraries.

---

* Virginia A. Walter, *Children and Libraries: Getting It Right* (Chicago: American Library Association, 2001), 88.

How else can one interpret an event such as a baby lapsit storytime with an attendance of, say, twenty-five, fifteen of whom are babies and toddlers, in a community that has roughly two hundred babies and toddlers? Those remaining 185 little ones are potential patrons, too, and yet are not to be seen at the library. And now this discussion highlights the expectation of extending professional service to babies, toddlers, and caregivers more fully, raising the bar yet again. Perhaps it is unfair to ask the children's services librarian to do even more by expanding to include quality service to these patrons (see the feature "Children's Libraries Are Community Places"). Perhaps, though, it is also unfair to deny babies and toddlers, the most voracious of learners, what has been rightfully theirs all along.

DEFINING GOOD LIBRARY PRACTICE

Within the profession, some have tried to qualify precisely what good library practice entails. Sandra Feinberg, Joan Kuchner, and Sari Feldman, for example, offer the following components of good library practice for children.[5] I have included a few comments about the application of each component to the provision of services to babies and families.

Good library practice
- Is individualized, varied, and cognitively and developmentally appropriate
  - » Every baby and toddler should be viewed as unique in her own way, respected for where she falls on the developmental time line, invited into the cognitive activity of mildly stimulating play, and worthy of the librarian's time and attention.

- Provides equitable access to a rich array of resources and learning opportunities
  - » Within the public library, every baby and toddler has the right to be able to access the board book collection through movement, curiosity, and independent volition. As much as possible, this collection should be kept relatively clean and physically safe, and books and other simple interactive elements, such as puppets and rattles, should be sturdy and safe.

- Reflects the strengths, interests, diversity, and needs of children and their families
  - » Almost by definition, every family *is* unique and diverse and presents its own strengths, interests, and needs. Because department-wide

service to babies and toddlers is relatively new to the profession and still plagued by the outmoded, stereotypical notion that families with babies and toddlers do not belong in libraries, the professional librarian should be willing to approach these families to offer assistance in providing services, especially because these families may be reluctant to ask.

- Fosters continuous individual development and encourages creativity, critical thinking, cooperation, and problem-solving skills from birth into adulthood
  » Children's libraries are already regarded as places in which library-appropriate play is used to encourage development, creativity, and other cognitive skills for other age groups. This play must also be extended in developmentally appropriate ways to babies and toddlers, with the goal of interactivity in mind. They should be freed from constraints yet safely ensconced and able to move about and have access to simple play materials, whether stationary or free-form, that are provided by the library.

- Implements appropriate policies, programs, and services
  » Individual library policies may need to be reviewed and revised with respect to the needs of this population. Programs, already strongly represented in libraries, need to continue to be extended to babies and include summer reading programs as well as, when possible, off-site events. Programs and services should also be reviewed and adjusted as necessary to accommodate this fast-growing and ever-changing population.

- Involves partnerships with parents, caregivers, and family service providers
  » Babies and toddlers, with their attending adults, require a service model that is inclusive of their collective as well as individual needs and should be perceived as such. Professionals should also become aware of, involved with, and active participants in local community children's health and development initiatives.

- Is flexible, accessible, and responsive to children and families
  » Because every family is different, and every day presents its own successes and challenges for this rapidly growing yet often vulnerable service group, quality professional interactions should demonstrate aplomb, acquiescence, compassion, and sensitivity.

Along with recognizing, practicing, and implementing these good service suggestions, librarians must be consider, evaluate, and perhaps adopt other aspects of service with regard to librarianship to babies and toddlers. There are publicity measures to address and continuing education avenues to explore. The librarian may also opt to develop research projects that further the profession's understanding of how physical, emotional, intellectual, and social library activities are benefiting this population. There are grants to be sought and advocacy efforts to be made. Policies may need to be reviewed and revised. These are exciting opportunities to consider, as they allow for a fresh emphasis and energy to permeate the world of children's services. And they give the librarian a fantastic excuse to engage more fully with this delightful population.

One way to rise to these challenges is to consult the International Federation of Library Associations and Institutions (IFLA). IFLA has produced a professional report entitled *Guidelines for Library Services to Babies and Toddlers*.[6] The guidelines include a checklist assessment tool designed to assist librarians in evaluating their current practices. This tool can be used to gauge where the local library currently stands, emphasize what it is accomplishing and doing well, and identify areas that may need more attention. With gracious permission, the IFLA checklist is included in this book and can be found in the appendix.

DREAMING BIG: THE FUTURE OF LIBRARIANSHIP TO BABIES, TODDLERS, AND CARE PROVIDERS

It just makes sense for the professional librarian to want to be a part of baby's brain development. Librarians as individuals are, for the most part, aware of these processes but as professionals have perhaps overlooked the enormous influence they can bring to bear on these little brains. Combining babies' vigorous growth with the fact that most communities in America have a public library advances libraries as institutions and librarians as facilitators of learning to truly great heights (see the feature "The Power of Poverty over Literacy"). This combination, fully realized, has the potential not only to promote healthy development but also to exert a positive cultural influence on its youngest patrons (and citizens), and for years to come. Why wouldn't we want to be a part of something *that* meaningful and wonderful?

So what would it look like for every community to have a librarian dedicated to serving *just* infants and toddlers, another librarian just for the preschool population, a third for the early grades, and, yes, even a fourth for the upper grades, similar to the way in which public schools are structured? Such a library would certainly look more adequately staffed. Outrageous, indeed. What may be more

The Power of Poverty over Literacy

The impact of poverty on today's children is enormous. According to a recent Children's Defense Fund report, "The United States, with the world's largest economy, has the shameful distinction of having the second highest relative child poverty rate among 35 industrialized nations." This finding is important specifically to librarians because poor parents have fewer financial resources and often experience more stress, and as a result their young children are less likely to be read to, spend less time talking to adults, and hear many fewer words each week than children from more affluent families. One study found that by age 4, high-income children had heard 30 million more words than poor children. Poor preschoolers are also less likely to be able to recognize letters, count to 20, or write their first names. Income-related gaps in cognitive skills can be observed in babies *as early as 9 months old* [emphasis added], and often widen with age. These disparities create an early disadvantage that is often hard to overcome.*

The public library, free and open to all, indeed has the potential to significantly alter these devastating statistics. The baby who begins life hearing up to 45 million words will be much more advanced and ready to embrace formal education than will the child who has heard only 15 million. If children's libraries are about anything, they most certainly are about words. This one remarkable and welcoming institution carries the potential to alter outcomes and elevate the poor, perhaps in very significant ways.

* Children's Defense Fund, "Ending Child Poverty Now," www.childrensdefense.org/library/Poverty Report/EndingChildPovertyNow.html.

outrageous is to think that one or two librarians can "do it all." Walter claims that "[i]t is unreasonable to expect that the same professional would have the skills and the time to serve all children in a community, from infancy through adolescence, as is the case in many libraries."[7] However, if the profession does not take itself seriously in these ways, disregarding the defending research, it runs the risk of becoming a trite reminder of days gone by—quaint, irrelevant, ineffective, and as passé as a card catalog. Serving all the children in the way just described would be optimal, but, given the knowledge of infants' rapid brain growth, libraries should consider providing such focused service most intensively to babies and toddlers.

Just imagine if the profession of children's librarianship had it all—ample personnel, funding, time, and the strong support of the administration and the community. What could the children's librarian bring to bear on the positive developmental trajectory of every child? More specifically, what if the vocation of librarianship allowed for, and even expected, a full-time position with fair compensation to exclusively serve babies, toddlers, and care providers?

Baby Steps

- Visit (daily?) local birthing units, introducing yourself as the baby's first professional education provider and offering a small gift and the library's contact information.
- Be available for spontaneous interactions that include infant play, book engagement, and conversations with, as well as readers' advisory for care providers.
- Advocate for the publication of books that will expand babies' and toddlers' growing vocabulary base.
- Create or provide programs specifically targeting this entire group, including topics of interest to parents and caregivers, such as breast-feeding or nutrition, as well as lapsit storytimes, perhaps even finding ways to integrate them.
- Collaborate with other public services providers for this population, attending professional meetings to stay abreast of current issues and concerns.
- Join other community agencies, such as local service groups, faith-based efforts, Help Me Grow, and state and local job and family services departments, to reach out to this population through in-home visits.
- Mentor a librarian joining the ranks. Explain various publications that will keep her informed of best practices, including those outside the field of children's librarianship.
- Read more about the history of children's librarianship—its heartfelt mission to children, how it has grown and changed over the years, and how it has succeeded so far—for fresh inspiration.
- Stay abreast of ongoing child development research. ZerotoThree.org is a wonderful gateway into this topic.
- Work with community groups that offer incentives to prospective parents who are at risk. For example, one local parenting clinic offers "baby bucks," which can be spent in the clinic's store, for clients who visit the library, take a tour, learn about the various resources, and meet with the children's librarian. Clients get "double bucks" if they apply for a library card!
- Host a local services and health fair, including professionals, intervention specialists, support groups, vendors, and other community entities interested in the welfare of families, car seat inspection, and the like.
- Become involved in, or at least make yourself more familiar with, local and state children's services agencies, faith-based services, or both.
- Visit an unfamiliar library. If possible, take a baby and a toddler with you. Experience the visit from the patrons' point of view. Discuss your experience with staff members. Brainstorm about how service could be improved.

- Send out personal invitations to young families not currently using the library. (Local faith-based groups, service agencies, and regularly attending library users can all be sources of referral.) Meet the families at the door and experience your library from the newcomers' perspective. Provide a small gift.
- Videotape a baby lapsit program (with parental permission), even if only in part. Revisit the video several times, studying the face and focus of one child at a time. Even a few minutes of this type of observation can be very informative and reaffirm that your efforts are meaningful and successful.

Big Steps

- Adapt the prerequisite course of library and information study, perhaps even at the undergraduate level, to require the library student to delve into such topics as infant and child development, family dynamics and diversity, emerging literacy, and basic social services.
- Take advantage of opportunities to remain updated through professional development not only within the profession but also through extended education in such topics as autism, communicable diseases, developmental delays, and other issues.
- Advocate for the latent power that children's librarianship possesses for this population, and for all children, at the state and national levels.
- Hire a full-time librarian with child development credentials to provide quality service that is specific to babies and toddlers and in which outreach, programming, on-the-fly interactions, and connections are made possible.

A CALL FOR ADVOCACY FROM ADMINISTRATORS

Children's librarianship can thrive within the library institution only through the defense, support, and dedication of a solid administration and board of trustees. Administrators, embracing such tenets as the *Library Bill of Rights* and *Code of Ethics*, set the tone, level of professionalism, and quality standards and expectations for their individual libraries. This book has opened the door for children's librarians, and libraries in general, to broaden their thinking and to consider and embrace methods for implementing real change (see the feature "Entities"). However, positive changes, such as those suggested here, can be accomplished only with the support and encouragement of administrators who can grasp the vision of, as well as the need and the urgency for, making these

Entities

M any of the problems faced by families of babies and toddlers are not limited to the poor. J. Ronald Lally, child advocate and one of the founders of Zero to Three: National Center for Infants, Toddlers, and Families, champions the right of all families to have "a national paid-leave program and universal well-baby care, screening, and follow-up services in the United States." Lally claims that if one missing support doesn't get them, another will. This was bad treatment of babies even before we understood that young brains depended on the attachments they formed in their first 9 months to provide them with necessary experiences. Given what we have learned about the important structuring of the brain that occurs during this period, it is foolhardy to withhold necessary services from babies. Without these support services, the chances of babies' brains getting through this period of development unscathed are greatly diminished. If we as a nation ignore the new information that science has provided us about the needs of the young brain, and continue to withhold help to families during the critical first 9 months of babies' lives, the neglect will be purposeful.*

---

* J. Ronald Lally, *For Our Babies: Ending the Invisible Neglect of America's Infants* (New York: Teachers College Press, 2013), 55.

changes. Without the full support of administration, efforts made by even the most committed librarians will be highly diminished. Ultimately, such weakened efforts trickle down to impact the already underserved and socially marginalized population of America's babies and toddlers. To really implement the deeply meaningful and lasting changes that are necessary, administrative backing is essential. What an opportunity! Library leadership possesses the power to invoke real cultural change for babies and toddlers and their families. As advocates and supporters of these important, and now fully recognized, library goals and missions, dedicated administrators can indeed raise the bar and lead the way for other institutions to follow in fully respecting and acknowledging this population, not only as future contributors to society but also as deserving human beings.

The continuing claim of inadequate dollars is tiring (see the feature "Funding and Other Excuses"). Money has been available for upgrading software, installing high-surveillance security cameras, purchasing very pricey databases, and so on. Some of these very expensive investments have come and gone and are now for sale at the Friends' bargain table. Yes, it is important to keep up with the technological advances and all the other wants and needs of a continually adjusting society. But those dollars are not necessarily allocated fairly, and it is usually the vulnerable babies and toddlers, who cannot speak for themselves, who are on the losing side of the funding equation. Administrators who believe in the importance of equitable services hold the power to reallocate some of those funding dollars more fairly and can choose to wield the power of their offices in more supportive ways.

Finally, administrators who truly respect and honor children's librarianship to babies, toddlers, children, and the families within their communities need to broadcast that message through better pay. Michael Sullivan, in *Fundamentals of*

Funding and Other Excuses

C hildren's librarians are part of the sociopolitical world. And they shoulder the weight of responsibility to provide everything they can for all the children in their communities. Today's librarians are teaming up with day-care centers, food service and delivery programs, the medical community, Head Start preschools, and any number of other locally based efforts to improve the conditions in which today's children are being challenged. These are true macro-service efforts and models, stretching the very meaning of children's librarianship, as these professionals continue their advocacy efforts. Children's librarians see profound needs up close and sincerely want to be agents of positive change, most especially as facilitators of reading. After all, it's hard to want to learn to read if one is hungry. However, the ability to address this responsibility is highly dependent on the choices and decisions made by administrators and other entities who hold the power and the purse strings.

One major challenge to ushering in any change, and especially one of this magnitude, is funding. J. Ronald Lally notes that in the larger world of politics, finance, and economics, "the total investment cost [of making better provision for babies and families] is so trivial relative to other budget items that the issue really isn't money at all. The issue is priorities."* Library administrators and others in library leadership have the power to consider their priorities in efforts to usher in a better system. This system would fully respect, honor, and provide thoroughly adequate library service to all children, especially as such service pertains to babies, toddlers, and their families and care providers, in whatever permutation it would take in local communities. Such an endeavor announces that our greatest resource, our children, is indeed worthy of deep investment. This model is not unrealistic and most certainly could be implemented. Rising to the challenge and setting a new standard might even be adopted by the wider culture. What a hopeful—and wonderful—idea.

* T. Berry Brazelton and Joshua Sparrow, foreword to *For Our Babies: Ending the Invisible Neglect of America's Infants* by J. Ronald Lally (New York: Teachers College Press, 2013), xiii.

Children's Services, reports that "children's librarians make less than other librarians because they are children's librarians."[8] Why? Is it because they work with children? Are the children themselves somehow less worthy of fairly compensated, quality service? At the very least, children's librarians should be equitably compensated. The profession itself most certainly expects and maintains lofty standards for quality, well-educated professionals, and rightfully so. This should be even more the case when considering the complexities involved in serving babies, toddlers, and families.

Attempting to attract fully trained, well-educated staff members who are not to be equally compensated sends a subtle message of condescension. This imbalance in pay also indicates that what children's librarians know, do, and provide is just not as valuable as what other professionals offer. Also, it sends the unsettling message that *those to whom children's services are provided* are just not as important as other patrons. Conscientious administrators may simply not see these inconsistencies or consider the implicit messages they send. Or perhaps they do not always understand the magnitude of the daily expectations of children's librarians. Perhaps because children, especially babies and toddlers, are so beguiling and sweet, those in higher library offices view service to them as more simplistic, and therefore less significant, than service to adult library patrons. In light of the discussions and arguments provided in this book, perhaps administrators can better grasp the magnitude of their own efforts when directly executing daily administrative duties toward this population.

To truly invoke lasting, powerful, and meaningful change for babies and toddlers, and indeed for all children, administrators are wholeheartedly invited to grasp the dream and pick up this crucial cause.

Baby Steps

- Support strict policies that mandate hiring well-prepared candidates.
- Help create the cultural perception of children's librarians as first education facilitators for babies and toddlers, just as pediatricians are first health providers.
- Equitably compensate children's librarians.
- Include children's librarians in administrative meetings with directors and board members because they provide a voice for this population.
- Hold roundtable discussions on what can be done in your local library.
- Invite the children's librarian and security and maintenance personnel to take a walk through the library, noting how the building itself is aiding or hindering service to families with babies and toddlers.
- Become more informed about children's librarianship in general and service to babies in particular.

- Advocate for the profession outside the library, speaking highly of the value and importance of what children's librarians do in general and what they are trying to accomplish for babies and families in particular.
- Interview staff members and evaluate their goodness-of-fit for public services and behind-the-scenes jobs, perhaps realigning job placement to everyone's mutual satisfaction.

Big Steps

- Use your considerable clout in the political arena to call attention to problems faced by families of young children and lobby for changes across the political landscape.
- Advance the work and the workplace of children's librarians in the larger political arena, lobbying for change.
- Allocate commensurate funding to children's services.
- Offer continuing education incentives to staff members who are willing to invest in additional coursework on the subject of human development.

DIGNIFYING BABIES AND TODDLERS WITH THE FOUR RESPECTS

Anne Carroll Moore, a pioneer of children's librarianship who served the New York Public Library from 1906 to 1941, developed the following Four Respects that are still embraced by children's librarians. Administrators are encouraged to review these "respects" and to examine their individual library's overt or covert prejudices. Again, to sharpen your focus, read the following with babies and toddlers in mind.[9]

The Four Respects
- Respect for children.
- Respect for children's books.
- Respect for children's librarians as an integral element in the library's organization.
- Respect for the professional status of children's librarianship.

Recognizing the potential, the patrons, and the profession for all that they are, could be, and should be, and then truly investing in them, ultimately depends on the deeply held convictions and assertive actions of administrators. Babies, toddlers, families, and children's librarians are counting on, maybe even crying out for, this deep level of support and commitment. The exhortation cannot be more heartfelt: be the champions for these patrons and the librarians who serve them, *on purpose*.

A FEW FINAL WORDS

Public library buildings are located in almost every city and town across the land. And professional children's librarianship is represented in these buildings. The profession itself has the power to move forward as a politically strong, unified, and caring voice, capable of making affirming changes for all children but especially for babies and toddlers. By seeking grants, lobbying for federal and state dollars, appealing to philanthropic entities, and educating and enlisting the backing of administrators, librarians can indeed find funding to implement these changes. In doing so, children's librarianship would be delivering the voice of the advocate, not only for the children but also for the profession and for the institution itself.

It is one of the convictions of our profession that all children's lives are enriched through an ongoing relationship with the children's librarian—a caring professional who provides meaningful learning experiences, especially with books. However, it cannot be emphasized enough that what children's librarians can be and do is profoundly important to the lives of children during the short period between birth and age two. It is no secret that being a children's librarian is a delightful occupation. It is joyful and enchanting to witness babies and toddlers in all their heartbreaking cuteness. But it is also very serious business. I encourage you to study the research and do what needs to be done in terms of place, practice, policy, and advocacy to make things better for every child, and especially for babies, toddlers, and their families, at the public library.

Notes

1. *Intellectual Freedom Manual* (Chicago: ALA Editions, 2010), 56–60.
2. S. R. Ranganathan, *The Five Laws of Library Science* (London: Edward Goldston, 1931), www.jdcc.edu/library/RFL.pdf.
3. Walt Crawford and Michael Gorman, *Future Libraries: Dreams, Madness, and Reality* (Chicago: American Library Association, 1995), www.jdcc.edu/library/RFL.pdf.
4. Virginia A. Walter, *Children and Libraries: Getting It Right* (Chicago: American Library Association, 2001), 123.
5. Sandra Feinberg, Joan F. Kuchner, and Sari Feldman, *Learning Environments for Young Children: Rethinking Library Spaces and Services* (Chicago: American Library Association, 1998), 90.

6. Kathy East and Ivanka Stricevic, *Guidelines for Library Services to Babies and Toddlers,* IFLA Professional Report 100 (2007), www.ifla.org/files/assets/hq/publications/professional-report/100.pdf.

7. Walter, *Children and Libraries,* 88.

8. Michael Sullivan, *Fundamentals of Children's Services* (Chicago: American Library Association, 2005), 9.

9. Julie Cummins, "More Than Meets the Eye," *School Library Journal* 45, no. 7 (1999): 27–29.

APPENDIX
IFLA Guidelines for Library Services to Babies and Toddlers

THE INTERNATIONAL FEDERATION OF LIBRARY ASSOCIATIONS AND INSTI-
tutions (IFLA), of which ALA is part, has created the *Guidelines for Library Services to Babies and Toddlers.* The guidelines are designed to assist libraries in gauging where they stand and how they may alter or change existing practices in order to provide better service to babies and toddlers. The introduction to the guidelines is provided in this appendix, along with the checklist tool and a web link to the entire report.

> The Guidelines are developed as a joint project (2006–2007) of all sections of IFLA Division of Libraries Serving the General Public, and coordinated by the Libraries for Children and Young Adults Section. The purpose of the guidelines is to help public libraries in various countries throughout the world to implement high quality children's services. They are intended as a tool for both trained and inexperienced librarians who have the responsibility of serving families with babies and toddlers. In featuring guidelines for the youngest users, this document supports the African proverb, "It takes a whole village to raise a child."[1]

CHECKLIST

For the best results, while using this as an assessment tool, within each box, mark the month and year which matches your progress: for example, if your library "needs to consider" including services to babies and toddlers in their mission statement, [commit to a specific date].

In the interest of serving BABIES and TODDLERS, parents, families, [care providers] and those who work with very young children, *every public library shall*:

1. *strive to provide* high quality children's services, support early learning, family learning, and life-long learning, seeing those services as important, and treated equally with, services for adults.

WHERE IS THE LIBRARY ON THIS CONTINUUM?

needs to consider	in planning stages	already implemented	achieving and evaluating

2. *include* service to BABIES (birth–12 months) and TODDLERS (12 months–3 years) in their mission statement.

WHERE IS THE LIBRARY ON THIS CONTINUUM?

needs to consider	in planning stages	already implemented	achieving and evaluating

3. *ensure* ease in obtaining library cards and library privileges.

WHERE IS THE LIBRARY ON THIS CONTINUUM?

needs to consider	in planning stages	already implemented	achieving and evaluating

4. *understand* the need for prominent signage, in both words and pictographs, to allow patrons independence in navigating library locations.

WHERE IS THE LIBRARY ON THIS CONTINUUM?

needs to consider	in planning stages	already implemented	achieving and evaluating

5. *provide* a clearly defined space dedicated to resources for BABIES and TODDLERS in all service locations, including mobile services and through delivery services.

WHERE IS THE LIBRARY ON THIS CONTINUUM?

needs to consider	in planning stages	already implemented	achieving and evaluating

6. *provide* access to library buildings for prams, strollers, wheelchairs, walkers, etc.

WHERE IS THE LIBRARY ON THIS CONTINUUM?

needs to consider	in planning stages	already implemented	achieving and evaluating

7. *select* and purchase materials for this audience, which support the literacy goal of "raising readers."

WHERE IS THE LIBRARY ON THIS CONTINUUM?

needs to consider	in planning stages	already implemented	achieving and evaluating

8. *provide* a welcoming environment that is comfortable and safe and conducive to early stages of development and learning.

WHERE IS THE LIBRARY ON THIS CONTINUUM?

needs to consider	in planning stages	already implemented	achieving and evaluating

9. *provide* a generous number of age-appropriate resources, in a variety of formats, including: toys, print, multimedia, technology and adaptive devices.

WHERE IS THE LIBRARY ON THIS CONTINUUM?

needs to consider	in planning stages	already implemented	achieving and evaluating

10. *provide* accessible materials and services for all regardless of ability.

WHERE IS THE LIBRARY ON THIS CONTINUUM?

needs to consider	in planning stages	already implemented	achieving and evaluating

11. *maintain* adequate staffing to offer reference and readers' advisory services, as well as to present programs.

WHERE IS THE LIBRARY ON THIS CONTINUUM?

needs to consider	in planning stages	already implemented	achieving and evaluating

12. *be responsible* for up-to-date educational opportunities and training programs.

WHERE IS THE LIBRARY ON THIS CONTINUUM?

needs to consider	in planning stages	already implemented	achieving and evaluating

13. *recognize* and address the diverse language and cultural needs of library users when acquiring resources and planning services.

WHERE IS THE LIBRARY ON THIS CONTINUUM?

needs to consider	in planning stages	already implemented	achieving and evaluating

14. *offer* age-appropriate programs and activities at various times of the day and various days of the week, to accommodate the variety of schedules kept by their clientele.

WHERE IS THE LIBRARY ON THIS CONTINUUM?

needs to consider	in planning stages	already implemented	achieving and evaluating

15. *provide* information fliers about library services throughout the community to attract the attention of everyone in the community.

WHERE IS THE LIBRARY ON THIS CONTINUUM?

needs to consider	in planning stages	already implemented	achieving and evaluating

16. *develop* partnerships with community groups and organizations to ensure the best facilities, services, and opportunities for the youngest members of the community.

WHERE IS THE LIBRARY ON THIS CONTINUUM?

needs to consider	in planning stages	already implemented	achieving and evaluating

17. *invite* presenters and speakers to enhance and expand a variety of topics of interest like parenting skills, preparing for kindergarten, etc.

WHERE IS THE LIBRARY ON THIS CONTINUUM?

needs to consider	in planning stages	already implemented	achieving and evaluating

18. *stimulate families and carers* to see the library as a frequent destination for learning and fun.

WHERE IS THE LIBRARY ON THIS CONTINUUM?

needs to consider	in planning stages	already implemented	achieving and evaluating

19. *publicize,* through a website and a variety of other means, including oral media, and in the languages of the community, the values of the public library as a rich and welcoming community resource.

WHERE IS THE LIBRARY ON THIS CONTINUUM?

needs to consider	in planning stages	already implemented	achieving and evaluating

20. *encourage* informal gatherings and discussions to nurture confidence-building and problem-solving skills for parents and carers.

WHERE IS THE LIBRARY ON THIS CONTINUUM?

needs to consider	in planning stages	already implemented	achieving and evaluating

21. *dedicate itself* to having a competent, sensitive, and culturally diverse staff, reflecting the community's population groups, to serve the multicultural needs of all users.

WHERE IS THE LIBRARY ON THIS CONTINUUM?

needs to consider	in planning stages	already implemented	achieving and evaluating

22. *have in place* evaluation tools and criteria to provide accountability of staff and offer required professional development opportunities in order to assure excellent service to all segments of society.

WHERE IS THE LIBRARY ON THIS CONTINUUM?

needs to consider	in planning stages	already implemented	achieving and evaluating

23. *strive for* adequate core funding to provide a FREE public library.

WHERE IS THE LIBRARY ON THIS CONTINUUM?

needs to consider	in planning stages	already implemented	achieving and evaluating

24. *keep abreast* of best practices from around the world and adapt and apply new ideas as they benefit the library in its quest for excellence.

WHERE IS THE LIBRARY ON THIS CONTINUUM?

needs to consider	in planning stages	already implemented	achieving and evaluating

Note

1. Kathy East and Ivanka Stricevic, *Guidelines for Library Services to Babies and Toddlers*, IFLA Professional Report 100 (2007), www.ifla.org/files/assets/hq/publications/professional-report/100.pdf.

REFERENCES

Baillargeon, Renée. "The Acquisition of Physical Knowledge in Infancy: A Summary in Eight Lessons." In *Blackwell's Handbook of Childhood Cognitive Development*, edited by Usha C. Goswami, 46-83. Malden, MA: Blackwell, 2003.

Berger, Sarah E., and Karen E. Adolph. "Infants Use Handrails as Tools in a Locomotor Task." *Developmental Psychology* 39, no. 3 (2003): 594–605.

Berger, Sarah E., Karen E. Adolph, and Sharon A. Lobo. "Out of the Toolbox: Toddlers Differentiate Wobbly and Wooden Handrails." *Child Development* (November–December 2005): 1294–307.

Bhattacharjee, Yudhijit. "Baby Brains: The First Year." *National Geographic* (January 2015): 57–77.

Brazelton, T. Berry, and Joshua Sparrow. Foreword to *For Our Babies: Ending the Invisible Neglect of America's Infants*, by J. Ronald Lally, xi–xiv. New York: Teachers College Press, 2013.

Campbell, Cen, Claudia Haines, Amy Koester, and Dorothy Stoltz. "Media Mentorship in Libraries Serving Youth." Association for Library Service to Children, 2015. www.ala.org/alsc/sites/ala.org.alsc/files/content/2015%20ALSC%20White%20Paper_FINAL.pdf.

Crawford, Walt, and Michael Gorman. *Future Libraries: Dreams, Madness, and Reality.* Chicago: American Library Association, 1995.

Cummins, Julie. "More Than Meets the Eye." *School Library Journal* 45, no. 7 (1999): 27–29.

Doyle, Christina S. *Information Literacy in an Information Society: A Concept for the Information Age.* Syracuse, NY: ERIC Clearinghouse on Information and Technology, Syracuse University, 1994. http://eric.ed.gov/?id=ED372763.

East, Kathy, and Ivanka Stricevic. *Guidelines for Library Services to Babies and Toddlers.* IFLA Professional Report 100 (2007). www.ifla.org/files/assets/hq/publications/professional-report/100.pdf.

Feinberg, Sandra, Joan F. Kuchner, and Sari Feldman. *Learning Environments for Young Children: Rethinking Library Spaces and Services.* Chicago: American Library Association, 1998.

Fogel, Alan. *Infancy: Infant, Family, and Society.* 4th ed. Belmont, CA: Thompson Learning, 2001.

Geidd, Jay. "The Teen Brain: Insights from Neuroimaging." *Journal of Adolescent Health* 42, no. 4 (April 2008): 335–43.

Ghoting, Saroj Nadkarni, and Pamela Martin-Diaz. *Storytimes for Everyone! Developing Young Children's Language and Literacy.* Chicago: ALA Editions, 2014.

Goswami, Usha C., ed. *Blackwell Handbook of Childhood Cognitive Development.* Malden, MA: Blackwell, 2003.

Gray, Peter. "The Decline of Play and the Rise of Psychopathology in Children and Adolescents." *American Journal of Play* 3, no. 4 (2011): 443–63.

Gross, Valerie J. *Transforming Our Image, Building Our Brand: The Education Advantage.* Santa Barbara, CA: ABC-CLIO, 2013.

Jha, Alok. "Why Crying Babies Are So Hard to Ignore." *Neuroscience* (October 2012). www.theguardian.com/science/2012/oct/17/crying-babies-hard-ignore.

Kagan, Jerome. *Galen's Prophecy: Temperament and Human Nature.* New York: Basic Books, 1995.

Library Design Associates. www.librarydesign.com/contact.html.

Listening and Spoken Language Knowledge Center. "Communication: How Babies Learn." www.agbell.org/Document.aspx?id=225.

———. "From Language to Literacy." www.agbell.org/Document.aspx?id=464.

———. "The Speech Banana." www.agbell.org/SpeechBanana.

Loudonville Public Library. www.loudonvillelibrary.org.

Ranganathan, S. R. *The Five Laws of Library Science.* London: Edward Goldston, 1931. www.jdcc.edu/library/RFL.pdf.

Snow, Charles W., and Cindy G. McGaha. *Infant Development.* Upper Saddle River, NJ: Prentice Hall, 2003.

Splashmakers. www.splashmakersllc.com/Splashmakers_LLC/Splashmakers_LLC.html.

Stern, Daniel N. *Diary of a Baby.* New York: Basic Books, 1990.

Therapy Center for Children. "Fine Motor Development and Handwriting." www.therapycenterforchildren.com/child-fine-motor-development-handwriting-suffolk-county.php.

Walter, Virginia A. *Children and Libraries: Getting It Right.* Chicago: American Library Association, 2001.

Zero to Three: National Center for Infants, Toddlers, and Families. www.zerotothree.org.

INDEX